Contents

Contents

Why I am Still a Catholic

To Rita Nicholson

*the best of Catholics and
a life-long inspiration*

Why I am Still a Catholic

Essays in faith and perseverance

Edited by
PETER STANFORD

continuum

CONTINUUM
The Tower Building
11 York Road
London SE1 7NX

80 Maiden Lane
Suite 704, New York
NY 10038

www.continuumbooks.com

First published 2005
Reprinted 2006

British Library Cataloguing in Publication Data
A catalogue record for this book is available from the British Library.

ISBN 0–8264–8577–1 (hb)
ISBN 0–8264–9145–6 (pb)

Typeset by BookEns Ltd, Royston, Herts.
Printed and bound in Great Britain by MPG Books Ltd, Bodmin, Cornwall

Foreword

One Holy, Catholic and Apostolic Church?

There are 1.1 billion Catholics in the world. In theory the Church we all belong to is as wide-ranging in its geographical spread as it is precise in its teachings. So – again in theory – there is little room for regional variations on the theme of what emerges from the Vatican. 'We believe in one Holy, Catholic and Apostolic Church' is the line we all chant in our own tongues every Sunday at mass during the Credo, whether we are reciting it in Aldershot, the Amazon or Addis Ababa.

Fine words. And that sense of being part of something so much bigger than any national boundaries is part of Catholicism. The reality, however, is that the huge economic, political and social differences between areas of the globe are reflected in how Catholics live their lives within individual societies. Yes, there is a template of beliefs and a liturgy that unites all Catholics, albeit no longer in a universal Latin, but the practice of the faith in daily life varies from place to place. Countries, continents and regions have their own distinct traditions within the broader Catholic family.

Here, following over 300 years of persecution after Henry VIII's break with Rome, modern-day Catholicism has developed its own particular flavour as a minority faith in a land that remains officially Anglican. This is, after all, a place where to be Catholic was to endure legal restrictions – on, for instance, the ownership of property – from the Reformation until 1829, where the restoration of the Catholic hierarchy in 1850 caused riots in the streets of London and outrage in the House of Commons. Catholicism was all but wiped out over those centuries of persecution. Only a few recusant families kept the flame of faith flickering in their priest holes. There are just three chapels where the Catholic mass has been celebrated without interruption since before the Reformation.

The Catholic Church has since been reborn here by successive waves of immigration – from Ireland, most notably, from continental Europe, and latterly from the rest of the world. However, until very recent times Catholics were still regarded as at best exotic and at worst something of a fifth column, owing allegiance to a foreign power, the pope. This stereotype is now, thankfully, fading. The late Cardinal Basil Hume, by the way in which he lead his Church on the national stage from 1976 until 1999, laid to rest many of the ghosts of the Reformation. Today's Catholics are more than ever before integrated into society and the establishment, largely middle class and, save for a few archaic laws to do with rights of succession to the throne, subject to no legal obstacles on account of their faith. They are to be found in all areas of national life, their belief usually unremarked upon.

Yet the history of hostility has left its mark. There are Catholics alive today, for example, who remember the bitterness of the sectarian violence of Liverpool in the middle years of the twentieth century. The composer James

Macmillan Scott caused headlines in 1999 when he spoke of continuing anti-Catholic prejudice at the heart of Scotland's political establishment. In such circumstances, domestic Catholicism has long had an instinct for hiding its light under a bushel, playing down or even ignoring the urge to proclaim the faith in favour of efforts to preach and promote toleration, integration and respect for other religions. In the political arena it has largely eschewed the confrontations with secular authorities on issues like abortion which have been the hallmark of the Church in other lands.

That feeling of apartness, of not being quite at home – whether real or imagined – gave Catholicism a distinctive identity in our country until the middle years of the twentieth century, what Cardinal Hume liked to call the fortress Church, closed in on itself, one step removed from national life. But with integration fresh questions have been posed. What does it mean to be a Catholic in a wealthy, rich, modern and largely irreligious society? If you are not eating fish on Fridays and following the letter of the law from Rome, then how are you distinct from anyone else? It is a question many Catholics struggle to answer.

The essays in this book explore how individual Catholics, across a range of ages from 31 to 86, and from a broad range of ethnic, social and theological backgrounds, relate to their Church today. Their answers illustrate the point that there are as many approaches as there are Catholics. Faith remains a very personal thing even in a universal Church. The individual's relationship with the magisterium – the teaching authority of a Church that remains keen on hierarchy – is rarely straightforward. What the contributors have in common, though, is that all, some admittedly after a battle which they relive here, remain Catholic, part of a Church that for so many in our secular, sceptical and scientific age is an anachronism, out of step with the world on issues like sexuality, gender, abortion, contraception and war and peace, but for Catholics themselves is what they have been given by God to work with.

Peter Stanford
Editor

A Global Caravan Site

Frank Cottrell Boyce, 44, is an award-winning scriptwriter whose credits include the Oscar-nominated Hilary and Jackie, 24 Hour Party People *and* Millions, *which was based on his novel of the same title. He lives in Liverpool with his wife and seven children.*

I'm too young to have been taught my catechism, a fact which I've always regretted. So I thought I'd write my own catechism, but it turned out that I didn't know enough and then the questioner turned nasty:

Why are you still a Catholic?
Why would I stop being a Catholic?

Well, where would you like me to start? Sex scandals? Financial scandals? Political scandals? Sexy political scandals involving money? *The Da Vinci Code*?[1] The Christian Brothers?
For some reason, they just don't bother me.

So you're a Catholic through mental lethargy? That's got to be a sin of omission.
I admit that as far as world Churches go, ours is probably the dodgiest but that's about the institution, not the faith.

1

The bombing of Dresden and Hiroshima, and the events of 9/11 all represent a misuse of aeroplanes. They might make you wonder just how beneficial aviation is, or how safe it is. What they don't do is make you doubt the possibility of flight. No one says, 'In view of what happened to the Hindenberg I no longer believe in lift.'

But you're a member of an institution – the Catholic Church. You are flying in the dodgy airship.

I'll take the risk.

Surely you can believe in God without buying into organized religion?

Actually you can't. God said – and He should know – 'wherever two or three are gathered together in My name'. Anyone who says different is just wrong.

Two or three is one thing. A big spiritual global corporation is another.

But you don't go to mass in a global corporation. You go in your parish. A parish is an amazing thing. Nowadays everyone is always fretting about social fragmentation. If you go to a Catholic parish on a Sunday, you'll see the opposite of that. You'll see people of all races and ages, and social class, coming together to share something really profound. And making a common identity for themselves. Every parish has the potential to be a neighbourhood Utopia.

So a bit like a static caravan site then?

I actually quite like caravan sites. The thing that's different with a parish is that you and your neighbours are joining yourselves to something genuinely global.

The caravan club has branches all over the world.
What I'm trying to get at is a sense of connection. A parish
can have a tiny geographical definition – maybe just a few
streets – but it's also probably twinned with somewhere in
South America or Africa. And at Christmas all the kids will
do those shoeboxes for Romania, and everyone will send
Christmas cards to prisoners of conscience in China or
America. So you have all these things that are forcing you to
look outwards, to connect with the world, at the same time
as making you spend time looking into your own soul. And
at the centre of all that is the mass, and at the centre of mass
is the consecration. So you've got all these people, all over
the world, concentrating on this single moment. That's a
powerful thought.

**Like in *Peter Pan* when everyone is supposed to clap
their hands to stop Tinkerbell dying?**
Except it's real.

No, it's like Tinkerbell.
I had this unusual experience. I was working on a project
about Caesar Augustus so I was reading lots of first-century
writing. And by chance, I ended up stuck with nothing to
read in a hotel room except the gospels and – even though
they were so familiar – it was like electricity. Because they
are nothing like, nothing remotely like, anything else that
was being written at the time. I know that as historical
documents they're full of contradictions and interpolations
because our attitudes to history have changed and so on.
But the thing that jumps out at you in the context of other
stuff from the period is that they are absolutely bursting
with authenticity. That someone would write about fisher-
men and prostitutes at that time – it's staggering. And that
things like St Peter's accent would be noteworthy. And that

amazing sense you get in the Passion narrative of a group of hicks coming into the city and creating panic and suspicion just by being there. The tension in the streets is palpable and so real.

I'm not disputing that something happened then. I'm saying it's just history. It's not mystically lingering like King Arthur asleep in his cave.
Christ is really present, in the present tense, in the mass.

No, He's not.
Yes He is.

If He is, it's in such an abstract way that it's meaningless.
It's the connection thing again. The structure of the Church connects you to people all over the world. The structure of the mass connects you to moments all the way through history. You're commemorating the Last Supper in a way that people have been doing almost since it happened. Sometimes – like in the cathedral in Syracuse – you're in a building that's been used for that purpose for thousands of years. Sometimes – like in the Sistine – you're doing it under the eyes of the greatest masterpieces of European art, which were created and put there just to help you concentrate. You're plugged into the dynamo of history.

I can't see that it's anything more than a kind of domestic Sealed Knot thing – a historical re-enactment. Like when out-of-work actors dress up as mill girls at Wigan Pier or New Lanark.
It's nothing like that. It's not just about an historical moment. It's opening a door into eternity. It's saying that this moment happened a long time ago but in another sense,

it is always happening. The Last Supper is always in the present tense. And you are present at it. So on a Sunday when everyone else is in IKEA or reading the paper, Catholics are sitting there experiencing the limits of linear time.

I defy you to take me through the physics of that.
Well, any physicist will tell you that time is much more complicated than it appears and that we have to dumb down our understanding of time in order to function.

You find me a physicist who will say that a single unique event, which happened 2000 years ago in Judea, is also continuously reoccurring in Pennsylvania and St Petersburg and Prescott.
Some things are hard to believe but that doesn't stop them being true. Black holes for instance. Or the amount of time evolution takes. It's difficult to get your mind around the idea that Jesus died for you personally. At the same time it's truer than anything else.

What!?!
It's the only thing I know that can give you a proper understanding of your place in the universe – that you're simultaneously an insignificant speck and also infinitely important and valuable. I meet people all the time who believe that they're utterly worthless and – especially in the film industry – I also meet people who think they exert more gravitational pull than the whole cosmos. It's actually very difficult to grasp that you're both things simultaneously but it is true. Not just theologically either. That's true in an evolutionary sense. In the broad scheme of evolution you're totally disposable but you might also be crucial because no one knows what's going to be important.

You're basically saying that being a Catholic is good for your self-esteem, like learning kickboxing.
When I was a child I lived in a fairly run-down area and later I lived on what should have been quite a boring estate. But in both places, I had access to this place of amazing beauty – the church – with its exotic smells and rituals and its direct line to Michelangelo and Leonardo and great poetry. Obviously that raised my expectations of life and that's great. But much more importantly it told me – it made me experience the fact – every fleeting moment is also an access point to the eternal, to another dimension.

When I was at primary school I remember collecting for the Holy Souls in Lent and then going to mass and watching the priest put the chalice in the tabernacle, and for some reason I had the impression that cash we'd raised was in the chalice and that when he put it in the tabernacle it went down in a kind of dumb waiter into purgatory, and they used the cash to buy themselves out. We lived in a block of flats at the time and there was a cupboard where the heating pipes ran. You could float bus tickets on the thermals. I remember thinking they ran down into purgatory.

Yes but you were wrong.
Anyone who's ever loved someone knows that that is true. You love someone – a spouse or a child – and you get used to them, irritated by them or whatever, and then the light will change and suddenly you'll see them as they were years ago and your sense of time gets more complicated because the past is still there and the future is sort of almost visible.

But like you said, anyone can experience that. It's there in Thomas Hardy's love poems and he was an atheist.
You can experience it without knowing what it is. Hardy

ended up believing all kinds of barmy things about fate and coincidence and stuff. It's like Chesterton said, when people stop believing in God, they don't believe in nothing, they believe in anything.[2] Like they believe shopping will make them happy or that they'll never die. Or wearing a brand name on your chest will make you cool, like members of a cargo cult.

Now you're sounding dogmatic and superior.
I love what my faith gives me and it's hard not to feel bad for people who've lost that. There's a special kind of time which I experience only in the supermarkets, or in reading the Sunday papers. It's sort of time in second gear – unpunctuated, steady, lacking in consequence. Like supermarket food: it doesn't come in seasons and it therefore lacks flavour, like those bloated, watery, Christmas strawberries. It's my faith that gives the world its flavour and its point. Even in the most mundane way – like fasting in Lent and feasting at Easter. It's to do with rhythm.

The rhythm method.
Ha, ha.

But you're still saying you're better than the rest of us. Scratch the surface and you find the old Inquisition is still there.
No. Whatever's gone on in the past, Catholicism is essentially the opposite of fundamentalism. Come on, it's a strictly monotheistic religion which is functionally polytheistic, what with saints and angels and Our Lady. Its aspirations are insanely high (weekly Communion with the Godhead) and its expectations are depressingly low (you'll need weekly Confession).

But there are doctrines that you have to believe in.
And they're true but they may not be the whole story. It's
like my computer. My computer is a very complicated
machine. It doesn't really contain filing cabinets, or have a
desktop or whatever. But if I'm going to get anything out of
it, I have to buy those metaphors. If I try to keep in mind
what's really happening in there, it won't be of any use to
me. It's important that your faith is useful.

**But you're saying you can only experience God
through the consecration, so you're excluding everyone who's not at mass.**
No I'm not. It's there in all creativity for instance. He made
us. We're His works of art. And when you're creating – I
mean when you're being truly creative, not when you're just
doing the job – you can feel a creative energy there that I
believe is exactly the same as the original creative energy.
You're carried beyond yourself into a space that must be
His. Every creative act participates in the original creative
act – which includes scoring an unlikely goal, or making an
amazing cake, as well as paintings and music and poems
and stuff.

Then why go to church?
I can only tell you how it is for me. I remember the first time
I went into Notre Dame in Paris. I remember having what
seems like a contradictory feeling – on the one hand of
stepping into a realm of impossible beauty and on the other
of coming home. I remember thinking, is all this for me?
And answering, yes it is. And it's also for everyone else. All I
can say is, that's how I'd like my children to feel. That's the
best I can do.

NOTES

1. Dan Brown, *The Da Vinci Code* (London: Corgi, 2003).
2. G. K. Chesterton, *What's Wrong with the World*, 1910).

Roots and Reins

Cristina Odone, 44, was editor of the Catholic Herald *for four years and deputy editor of the* New Statesman *for six. She is a columnist for the* Observer *and has written two novels. She lives in London with her husband and daughter.*

As a child, I used to spend my summers in a small village in northern Italy. Here my beloved great-aunts, Meri and Pina, took care of a brood of us cousins. My great aunts, childless widows both, were extremely devout, and although they did not insist that we accompany them to mass every morning, we were marched there on a Sunday at 11 am every week.

I was not, I confess, the most attentive among the congregation. I would lose myself in day dreams prompted by the stained-glass windows with their medieval saints, or in contemplation of the glossy plaits of my older cousins in the pew in front. The villagers too kept me occupied: elderly women, bowing and murmuring, their mantillas concealing their faces; stocky farmers wearing their Sunday best, surrounded by their wives and children.

One villager in particular always drew my gaze. She was a good-looking, middle-aged woman, whose sophisticated, city clothes betrayed the summer visitor. My great aunts would greet her on our way into church, but she never visited us, nor did they ever speak of visiting her. This alone might not have roused my curiosity, were it not for the fact that I had noticed something altogether more disturbing about the lady: she never took Communion.

I knew from my catechism classes that the sacraments were essential to a Catholic life. There is no greater gift than to share in the body and blood of Christ, and to be forced to forego such a blessing spoke of a great sinner indeed. While everyone else would queue up, the elegant woman would kneel, face buried in her hands. Sometimes I fancied I saw her shoulders quiver, and once, when she pulled her face away from her cupped hands, I saw plainly the tears on her face.

Full of pity for this sorrowful, if sinful, stranger, I asked my great aunts at lunch what had happened to the lady in church that kept her from taking Communion. 'She is divorced', replied my Aunt Meri. And then she pursed her lips and set her jaw in a way which told me further discussion was forbidden.

Some 30 years later, I find myself reliving the stranger's pain. I am married to a divorcee. As I will not give up my marriage to Edward, I recognize that mine is a sin for which there is no absolution. I know that this makes me the unwanted guest at the Eucharistic banquet. As a result, the weekly mass has been transformed into a very different experience from the comforting one I grew up with.

The tension begins as the church fills with the closing words of the Creed – 'and the life of the world to come, Amen.' It mounts as the priest intones the words of the offertory and with a deliberate, almost dramatic, gesture removes the veil from the chalice. The priest lifts the bread, and the habitual struggle takes hold of me. I yearn to be part of this, but know that I may not. The extraordinary

rite with which we celebrate God as man, and with which
Mother Church folds the faithful into her embrace, excludes
me. I stay in my pew, a spectator, as others queue up to take
communion and seal their membership in my Church. I
must stand by, trying hard as I might not to feel as forlorn as
the woman I used to spy in our village church.

I love my husband, the father of my child. He is the soul
mate that I spent years waiting for, the loving presence I
had hitherto only dreamed of. When I met him, Edward
was separated from his wife. He was unhappy, I was lonely:
we plunged headlong into loving one another. Surely
something that brought such happiness to two people –
and to those dearest to us – could only be a good thing? Yet
from the beginning, as I felt my world turn upside down, I
realized the consequences of our union. As a Catholic, I had
two options: annulment or exclusion. I was tempted by
annulment: it smacked of casuistry, but it promised a guilt-
free, hitch-free marriage and the sacraments. Yet I was torn:
annulment combines everything I find disappointing in the
Catholic hierarchy's approach to problems. Annulment
pretends that a marriage never took place; it tries to push
the troubled union under the carpet, as if by not recognizing
it, the whole relationship would – puff! – go away. This
turning-of-a-blind-eye has been echoed, disastrously, in the
Church's approach to paedophile priests: rather than
admitting that one of their own is guilty of a gross affront
to society's most vulnerable, the hierarchy shuffles priests
suspected of abuse from parish to parish. It is a dreadful,
irresponsible policy.

A terrible truth – whether it be a broken marriage or a
paedophile priest – will not disappear simply by wishing it
away. And where is the pastoral care in shying away from
rather than confronting such grave issues? How does a priest
deal with the parishioner who says his child has been abused

by another priest? How does a priest answer the parishioner who asks, 'Father, can I be forgiven for walking out of a marriage that broke my spirit'? What does he say to the pious woman who begs forgiveness for divorcing the man who battered her body or drank away their earnings?

At the dawn of the twenty-first century, these are not lone voices: with one in three marriages in Britain ending in divorce, the proportion of Catholics who are divorced or entering relationships with divorcees is today far higher than ever before. Their spiritual guardians cannot simply pretend that divorce is something that will go away. As in the case of the paedophile priests, failure to address problems can lead to confusion, torment and, worse, harm. Much better, surely, to shine a light of faith upon the issue and examine it thoroughly.

I have lived through an annulment and its aftermath. I am the daughter of divorced parents. When my father decided to remarry a Catholic, he sought and obtained an annulment of his marriage to my mother. For my brother and me, born of this 13-year marriage, the notion that our parents' union had never taken place seemed preposterous – and hurtful. How could I revisit such pain and confusion through my two stepsons?

This left me to contemplate a fate I'd never imagined: exclusion from the Eucharist. I spoke to several priests before Edward and I got married. Many were remarkably liberal: in their eyes God would not be offended by a loving union that had involved no betrayal and would inflict no pain. If it was all right with my conscience to continue taking Communion, who would bar me from the host?

Yet the trouble was that my conscience would allow no such flexibility. I had been brought up believing that divorce was evil, and that to marry a divorcee was to fall from grace and break with the faith. I could not now blithely overlook my catechism or rearrange my beliefs and continue as before.

How then can I still be a Catholic? I am banned from the central experience of Catholic practice. Why do I keep holding on?

When Thomas Aquinas described the Church, he spoke in terms of roots and reins. Certainly the Church has given me roots. An Italian brought up mainly in America, who studied in Britain and worked for a few years in America before finally settling down in Britain, I am hard pressed to describe 'home'. Hard pressed that is until I close my eyes and hear a choir singing the Latin words to the Credo, or fill my lungs with incense, or bask in the multi-coloured reflections of a stained-glass window. At mass – lulled by well-loved hymns and the familiar words of the liturgy, comforted by the ancient rituals of the service – I feel that I belong.

Yes, the Church roots me: the congregation is my community; and the tenets of my faith are my foundation. I would be shaky and vulnerable, always flapping and dithering, were it not for the solid certainty with which my faith provides me. I know who I am and whom I must obey; I know that I am as precious, in the eyes of God, as the woman I have met at the office and the man I run from at the drinks party.

This sense of Catholic identity is precious. We live in an unforgiving culture, which places tremendous pressure on the young to be beautiful, on the old to look young and on everyone to be successful. To be found wanting on any of these scores is to risk pariah status – whether that means being teased in the school playground or being excluded from the 'A' party list. This is a materialist culture – not only materialistic in its belief that money can buy every-thing, but materialist in that it believes only the concrete is of value and there is nothing beyond the here and now.

This viewpoint is all engulfing. It presses on us from all sides, from the pages of the newspaper we read at breakfast, through the billboards we drive past on our way to work, to the conversation we overhear at the wine bar. After such 24/7 messaging, it is difficult not to view your success in terms of a promotion and your failure in terms of a larger dress size.

But against the backdrop of my faith, this empty and limited perspective seems highly resistible. I know that I am more than the sum total of my IQ or my bank balance. Again and again, Catholic teaching affirms humanity's sacred status. You can turn back to Augustine and Aquinas, and more recently to Newman and Jacques Maritain, to find humanity and the world it inhabits described as infinitely wonderful, filled with grace and endless hope – a true reflection of God's boundless love.

To this end the writings of Pope John Paul II provided a powerful, contemporary witness: from the poor of the Third World to the unborn child, to the Iraqi civilians, he championed human beings as God's much-cherished creation. Every living being was dear to Him; to treat any human being with anything less than respect was to risk offending our Lord.

St Thomas spoke of reins, as well as roots. Reins are commonly regarded as a list of prohibitions. 'Thou shalt not' seems to preface so much of what we are taught, that the negative imperative often seems to be choking the very life out of our faith. But to rein in a horse is not to immobilize or castrate him; it is to guide him.

Equally, the reins that our Church holds are to guide us to fulfilment, rather than block or disempower us. Outsiders see these rules as nothing but an old-fashioned ban on contraception, abortion and homosexual relationships. The Catholic is the killjoy Church, the one that, to the outsider, focuses all its fire and brimstone on contemporary sexual conduct.

In fact, the Church's guidelines are not sex-obsessed. If papal pronouncements on condoms and same-sex marriages grab headlines, that is because sensationalism sells papers, and talk of charity, humility and forgiveness does not. The Church's guidelines are not confined to the bedroom, but cover whole areas of daily experience, from our interaction with colleagues to our attitude to the beggar in the street.

Today, when we regard democracy as the supreme good, the notion of our being bound by rules and regulations drawn up by an unelected leader smacks of authoritarianism. It is simply not the accepted way of the twenty-first century. Worse, many of these rules actually quash the ego and ask us to humiliate ourselves; they demand that we share our hard-earned good fortune and forgive our harshest critics. People simply shake their heads and walk away. As GK Chesterton put it: 'the problem is not that Christianity has been found wanting but that it has been found difficult and not tried at all.'[1]

Several times I've been brought up short, as I consider taking an action or uttering a word, and realize that I am being tugged back from action by those invisible reins. Yes, I bridle at the thought of my freedom being circumscribed – yet imagine a life where we have no reins and wander about doing as we please, automatically satisfying our every wish, ignoring our responsibilities or others' needs. Surely this is a dangerous – and ultimately dull – prospect.

'Your Church demands a great deal of you', I remember one atheist colleague remarking. I should have answered that yes, it does, because it confers so much upon us. I can look to the Church for my identity and for a *vade mecum*.

I can also find in the Catholic faith a celebratory dimension, which is often absent from other religions. I remember listening to some eminent theologians, representing many denominations and many corners of the world, as they discussed the extraordinary delight that rings out in some of the passages of the Old and New Testaments and in particular the Psalms. Some of the learned scholars felt this joyful spirit was at odds with much of the tone of the Bible – and with much of the preaching they heard each week in their own churches. These theologians discussed their Church's vision in terms of fear of divine retribution, an oppressive sense of sin and an emphasis on the anguish of the Passion rather than the glory of the Resurrection. I did not recognize in their dour words the ringing gratitude and unstinting delight that I associate with my faith. I do not view life as a vale of tears, and sorrow as the only way to experience holiness.

The Catholic Church is about raising our voice in chorus to celebrate our Father's glory as well as setting out to retrace the steps of the via Crucis. It is about Mary, who relishes our Lord's words, as much as about Martha, who does her duty so admirably. It is, in short, about recognizing that amidst the gloom and doom, there are heart-warming incidents, special moments and much-loved people. This is the fullness of life, and our tremendous gratitude for it finds expression in a faith that accommodates Raphael's beautiful Madonnas and fabulously colourful Holy Day processions with the monk's spartan cell and the Lenten fast. Joy may not be an emotion exclusive to Catholics, but its expression lies at the very heart of many of our rituals.

When I was appointed deputy editor of the *New Statesman* in 1998, I remember someone warning me that religion and politics are both all-consuming passions and in both there is always the risk of losing faith. I replied that although I could imagine falling out with New Labour, I could never conceive of losing my Catholic faith.

I was right. My political affiliations have grown more tenuous after my disappointment in some of that government's policies, but despite suffering from my new status as a 'non-sacramental Catholic', I have not lost my faith. I am tested each week, it is true. I must humble myself and recognize that, having breached a promise, I am not worthy to receive Him.

Yet I still attend the mass, I still follow the tenets of my faith, and I still teach my daughter that she is a Catholic. I live in the hope that, just as Cardinal Newman argued, theology is not 'a finished subject or a closed chapter',[2] the door to my Church is not firmly shut. The convert cardinal saw the Church as a living organism, and its doctrine as ever expanding. Each generation of Christians, he taught, was called upon to increase the intellectual capital of the tradition.

My fervent wish is that this generation of Catholics, many of whom will have experienced divorce first hand, will be invited to contribute to debates within the Church about the issue. Already there are signs of the Church reaching out to this growing number in the community – there are national and diocesan associations that bring together Catholics whose marriages have broken down. What we need is for such groups to keep a constant line of communication open with the hierarchy so that priests and bishops may come to recognize quite how painful and difficult our lot is. In this way, perhaps, our theology will develop and – who knows – come to embrace those of us who at present must feel unwelcome.

I think I know what the woman of my childhood summers must have felt; but I also know that I will not allow myself to give in to her despair. I will go on hoping for a reconciliation.

NOTES

1. G. K. Chesterton, *What's Wrong with the World* (1910).
2. Cardinal Newman, *Apologia Pro Vita Sua* (1864).

A Little Bit of Grit

Cherie Booth, 50, is a barrister specializing in human rights and employment law. She was appointed a QC in 1995 and is patron of many charities. She is married to Tony Blair and has four children.

There are, I suppose, two main reasons why I'm still a Catholic. The first is that I was born and brought up as one and have never reached a point in my life when I have seriously considered giving it up. There is that basic family pull which, in its simplest form, means that to stop would be to let down my grandmother who brought me up as a Catholic.

The second reason is to do with being a parent. When I had my children, I wanted them to be Catholics too. Part of it was inevitably wanting them to think like me, but also I didn't want them to be too comfortable. I wanted them to have that little bit of grit in their lives that is there in Catholicism, especially in its social teaching.

Of course, like many Catholics in this country, I have doubts about some of the positions taken by the Church as an institution – for example, on contraception or the role of women. But I am not one of those who believe that the only response is to walk away because you have a different viewpoint. I have been taught that you should stay and try to change things.

It's like the Labour Party in the early 1980s. I wasn't happy with the way it was going so I tried to help change it from within. Thankfully, we won that battle. And though the pace of change in the Catholic Church can seem slow, I believe that there are many people in this country – and not just in the laity – who are convinced of the need for it. That message, however, is not yet fully accepted in the Vatican. But, then, the Church isn't just the Vatican. It is about all of us, the people of God as the Second Vatican Council put it.

Since Tony became leader of the Labour Party, my Catholicism has become much more public than I'd ever expected. It never occurred to me to hide it. It is, after all, what I am and a part of my life. I don't think people are really bothered by it one way or the other. But sections of the press seem to have a different view. At times they have tried to make an issue over the choice of Catholic schools for our children, for instance, or claimed that Tony was about to convert because he wants to attend a church service with his wife and children who are all Catholics. I can only think they choose to do this because they believe Catholicism is a vote loser. I think that they have got this wrong – and see the more relaxed attitude of the public at large as a positive sign about the health of our society.

There was, of course, prejudice in the past. At Chequers, for example, there is a painting of an order set up by Queen Elizabeth I to persecute Catholics. I sometimes point that out to guests as a symbol of how far our society has come. And, in Liverpool where I grew up, there have certainly been sectarian divisions. They had a major impact, for example, on my grandmother. The great love in her life had been a Protestant but they hadn't married because both families were against it. When she did eventually marry, my grandfather converted to Catholicism.

As I have said, it was my grandmother who brought me

up as a Catholic. Her cousin was our parish priest. Her brothers had two sons who were priests, one who was only three years older than me. I wouldn't say that she was a terribly pious woman, but Catholicism was just part of our daily life. That is what we were.

By the time of my childhood in Liverpool, the sectarian rivalry of the past had pretty much faded but you still lived, in some ways, quite separate lives – much more so than nowadays. We lived, for example, in a fairly Catholic neighbourhood. When I went to Brownies and Guides, it was to a Catholic troop. My schools were all Catholic. We convent girls from Seafield mixed with the Catholic boys from St Mary's College in Crosby, but not with those from Merchant Taylors, the nearby non-Catholic school.

I remember, too, there was some faint rivalry when I was around five or six between those of us who went to the Catholic primary and those who attended the local non-Catholic school. There was a bit of name-calling, but it was very minor. Perhaps because my mother herself wasn't a Catholic, I was less affected than others.

Things began to change with the Second Vatican Council, which took place while I was at school. As teenagers, we were encouraged to put into practice its ecumenical reforms, and so we were sent out to the local Congregationalist and Anglican churches as part of religious studies. That was as far as inter-faith stretched back then. It was a big thing just to attend a Church of England service. It is tremendous that so many more barriers have now been broken down.

Through school I got involved in the Young Christian Students, a Catholic organization that had grown out of the Young Christian Workers. It was all about applying faith through social work or, as I personally came increasingly to see it, through socialism. As part of Young

Christian Students we'd meet with the boys from St Mary's (which was, of course, an added attraction) and have discussions about ethical issues. We'd play our guitars and have masses in the round or outdoors which were full of sharing and 'Bridge Over Troubled Water'. We thought we were very radical and would change the world. We put on 24-hour fasts in the city centre for the Third World, and over the summer holidays would organize a playgroup on a housing estate in Kirby, one of the more needy areas of Liverpool.

My Catholicism certainly contributed to the development of my own political views. My Catholicism comes from my background and so do my politics. We were a working-class family. Catholicism and socialism were the ways we thought things were going to get better. Catholicism gave us the aspiration that we should all be equal.

Though I now recognize the connection between Catholicism and the aims of the human rights legislation I work with as a lawyer, I'm afraid that my faith played only a negative role in my choice of career. I had become quite rebellious towards the end of my time at convent school. While the nuns thought it was good that we should strive to do well in our exams, they seemed to believe there was a limit to how far we should go in our careers. Their ambitions for us seemed to me to stretch about as far as doing a bit of teaching and then giving it all up to be a Catholic wife and mother. Though there is nothing wrong with that, I personally didn't find the prospect too appealing at the age of 18. I had loved history at school and would have liked to study it at university, but thought that would inevitably mean I'd end up being a teacher waiting to be asked to be a Catholic wife and mother. So I chose law, as much, I suspect, to annoy the nuns as anything. They were also deeply, deeply unhappy about my choice of university. They saw the London School of Economics (LSE) as a den of iniquity.

I remember even then thinking this was a contradiction in Catholic teaching. On the one hand, we were all told we must make of full use of our talents. On the other, there seemed to be all sorts of assumptions based on the notion that women were somehow inferior. By the age of 15, I'd spotted this and thought it was wrong. And still do. Women still do not get due respect in the Church which is why, in the opinion of many people, it gets some things wrong, like its teaching on contraception.

Just before I set off for London, I realized I hadn't filled in the forms for student accommodation. There was a last-minute panic and I was found a place in a convent in Notting Hill. It was part of a Catholic teacher-training college. I stayed there for about three days, all the time thinking I've spent enough of my life in a convent already without spending another three years in one. Then I managed to talk my way into an LSE hall of residence. Once there my involvement with anything to do with Catholicism or even Christianity lessened. When I went home, I'd still go to mass, but not when I was in London. I did so without any particular guilt. I didn't consider I was rejecting the whole thing. Perhaps I should have. But one of the things that distinguishes Catholicism is that there is no real sanction beyond your conscience. It talks of excluding people, but it is really a self-regulating institution in that people choose to exclude themselves from the sacraments if their lives diverge from the teachings.

And being Catholic can mean holding a set of views that to outsiders might seem contradictory. So I'm a feminist but I have an enduring soft spot for the Virgin Mary. She, for me, is an important part of Catholicism because I passionately believe there is no more important role in life than motherhood. I admire her self-sacrifice, her ability to accept God's will and her trust in Him.

I sometimes find trusting in God hard. It goes against my strong instinct that we have to work dilemmas out for ourselves. Lawyers often feel that if only everyone else allowed us to sort out the world's problems, everything would be fine because we're so logical and sensible. But faith is not just about logic. It is about something more fundamental and far more personal.

Even in those student years I was never uninterested in my Catholic faith. It remained a part of me, who I was. I never felt I left the Church. But, like many others, it was once I became a parent that I started to go back to mass regularly again. I wanted my children to be brought up as Catholics, with a sense of religion and the routine of religion.

What I found when I did start attending mass regularly, with the children, at our local church – and what remains a strong attraction for me in Catholicism – is a sense of community. That was increased because the children all went to the local parish primary school. And through the church and through the school, particularly in the mixed area where we lived, we came across people from a wide range of backgrounds and jobs. They certainly weren't all lawyers or politicians. It was a real community. The surprise was how, once you belong to such a community, you end up organizing the music, doing the readings and acting as a school governor. Before long, you appear to others as a fine, upstanding member of the parish. I wanted to pinch myself and used to think 'what, me? I'm the naughty girl'. I wonder what the nuns who taught me would think.

Even though my older children are grown up, I still find that this sense of community above all else draws me to church. It probably always will. Living in Downing Street, of course, makes it harder to find because of the security arrangements that have to surround us. But I look back on our time in a parish in north London as among the happiest in our family life and I look forward to getting back to that one day in the future.

Put to the Test

Shaun Edwards OBE, 38, made a record eleven appearances in Rugby League's Challenge Cup Final and was on the winning side on eight occasions for his hometown club, Wigan. The legendary Great Britain international now works as a coach at London Rugby Union team, Wasps.

My younger brother was killed in a car crash on 8 February 2003. Billy Joe was only 20 and was making his name in Rugby League in Wigan. There were just the two of us and despite the age gap we were close. He was a likeable kid. Most brothers don't get on that well, but we did. He was different from me, a lot more laid back and very happy-go-lucky, but he was my mate.

It was one of those moments when you wonder if there really is a God. My immediate reaction was to tell God to get lost – for want of a better word. I was just like Job in the Old Testament. It seemed too much. I didn't really mean it, though. Sometimes it can help to have a go at God. In fact since Billy Joe's death I have found myself working much harder at my Catholic faith.

Time doesn't heal. We are still learning how to cope. Whatever pain I was feeling, though, it was worse for my mother. I have had to be strong for her. She is totally devastated. I really don't know how people who don't believe in anything handle a situation like that. Just the thought that I might see Billy Joe again, that one day we might all be together as a family, is what keeps me going. For people with no faith, it must be unbearable.

My mum is very close to God. I often think the closer you get to God, the greater the tricks that the Devil plays on you. They get more and more harsh to try and turn us away from God. You see that a lot in the lives of the saints. They have a huge amount of suffering. I do believe that there is that negative influence out there, whether you call it the Devil or whatever, and it's there when people get close to God. They are being put to the test. We as a family have been put to the test by losing Billy Joe.

Both my parents are Catholics. My mother's brother is a priest and her other brother went to seminary, but he came out without completing the course. So I was brought up a Catholic – Catholic school, church every Sunday, and sometimes during the week. It was just what was expected.

Both of my grandmothers worked at the priest's house – as my own mother does now at St Mary's in Wigan, the parish I grew up in. Being around the church was part of my young life. I used to go and help my granddad when I was five or six to fill up the fires at the church with coal. He also used to clean it – even though he was Protestant. I think he eventually turned Catholic but he wasn't born one. In fact both my grandfathers turned Catholic.

When my mum was a child growing up in Wigan, there had been hatred between Catholics and Protestants. At least that is what she used to tell us. There was nothing as intense when I was a kid – a bit of name-calling, 'Proddy dogs and all that', but nothing more serious.

When you become an adult, you tend to make up your

own mind about how you feel about the Church. I'm certainly not one for separatism when it comes to religion. I've no time at all for the old idea that one way, the Catholic way, is better than any other. Moslems, Hindus, Protestants, they can all find God. Putting any religion above another is wrong. It is what causes war and hatred in the world. I believe passionately that we have one benevolent God who is for all races and all human beings. That seems to me to be the true Catholic attitude to have. I believe in the brotherhood of man. I don't go along with this 'us and them' attitude. I'm a big believer in 'we'.

I can't say I've always lived a totally Christian life in all aspects. I have had my faults and failings and still do. In anyone's life, there are always going to be times when your faith is more intense, but I've never lost it in the important things – like the fact that there is an afterlife. That has helped a lot since Billy Joe died.

I've started to meditate. I'd never done that before. Most people don't see that as a Catholic thing to do, but when I looked into it, I found that the likes of Saint Francis of Assisi were heavily into meditation. So it's not just for Buddhists or Hindus. There is a link with Christianity, which, because of how I was brought up, helps. And it is just another example of how all religions are inter-linked, how different messages and routes lead us to the same light.

I'll meditate for example on all the mothers in the world who have lost a child and I find some comfort. And I pray more than I used to before Billy Joe's death. As a kid, I used to say a prayer before playing a match. 'Thank you God for the chance to play. Please make sure that no one gets injured.' Maybe when I was 11 or 12 I'd add, 'please let me score a try', but I soon realized that God's blessing on me was the strength of mind and body to play. The rest was up to me. I never really stopped praying, but I do it more now.

And there's more of a commitment to my faith. It is more than just going to church at weekends.

As I get older, my attitude to Catholicism changes. It's not that I'm rebelling against it and its teachings. That would be the wrong word. It is rather that I don't like this attitude that you are not to question. If you do question and still you believe, or you come through still questioning, then your faith will be stronger. That old idea that if you don't believe in everything the Church says you'll be damned in hellfire permanently is not something I go along with.

I see a lot of signs of change in the Church today. Change for the better. I'm not judging priests or people in the past or saying 'these priests told people what to do and they were wrong'. That was their way of doing it then. It's not for me to sit in judgement. One important part of being Catholic is not to be too judgemental.

I'm a down-to-earth person and my Catholicism is very practical. When something happens like Billy Joe's death, it would be easy to become bitter. To avoid those feelings, we have to try and help as many people in whatever way we can. I find if I feel down or depressed and then I go and help someone else, it picks me up.

I've always had an idea about working abroad as a helper, but at the moment it's just an idea because I have a small son, James, here in London and he needs me. It's there though in the back of my mind to do a bit of voluntary service one day.

When I retired from Rugby League in 2000, I helped out occasionally at a soup kitchen run by Mother Teresa's Missionaries of Charity on Ladbroke Grove in west London. I'd do the night run with them. I'm not making out I was a saint to do it. I just wanted to help and I had time because I'd stopped playing. And occasionally having me around helped diffuse some tense situations.

Since Billy Joe's death I have started to go back there. I don't want to make too much of it, to sound holier-than-thou. It's just for an hour or two every week or two. They don't do the night runs any more. There is less demand. But being there helps put things in perspective, to look at life at the sharp end. I like being around the nuns. They are so innocent. They never question anything. If something comes from the Pope, that's enough for them. There is a Catholic way to do things and they do it.

I admire them and I wish I was more like them, but I'm not. I think a lot more about faith now than I ever have and ask many more questions. On some issues, the Catholic Church has its ideas and I have mine. I walked out of church the other week. The priest was preaching about the war in Iraq and he said the people to blame for the suffering were those in this country who had voted our government in. I just thought, I'm not listening to this. It was the first time I've ever done it. I came back in, of course, once he'd finished and did the rest of the mass.

He was only one person. It was his view. And his view is not going to put me off something that is simply a part of my life. Jesus is my way to salvation. I do read about other ways, other faiths, and I'm amazed at how their messages are all the same. But Catholicism is what I have grown up with, and its message of love and compassion to other human beings. That's it as far as I'm concerned. That's why I'm still Catholic.

The Ant on the Face of
the Computer

Bruce Kent, 75, is vice-president of Pax Christi and CND. He spent 29 years as a Catholic priest before retiring in 1987 to continue his work in the peace movement. He lives in north London with his wife, Valerie.

Why am I still a Catholic? It's an odd sort of question. It sounds as if the onus is on me to explain why I stay where I am. But perhaps not all that odd. For a wide variety of reasons many of my generation have given up. Many of their children and grandchildren have no involvement with the Catholic Church despite Catholic baptism and Catholic education. So maybe I do have to explain myself. It might even be an encouragement to other members of my community to whom the Church at times seems so embarrassingly unattractive.

There seem to be two parts to the question. Why stick with religious faith at all when a tolerant agnosticism seems to satisfy so many? And why not join another Church – or faith community, to use the respectable language of the day?

Agnosticism, and still less atheism, don't suit me. As I grow older, I find it more and more difficult to look at our world without passionate curiosity and ongoing wonder. From invisible dividing cells to endless galaxies, from mountain tops to modern communications, from human love to art and music, I sit back in awe. Psalm 8 rings in my head on a daily basis. 'What are we that you should keep us in mind, men and women, that you care for us?'

All our lives we pursue rationality: cause and effect. Why did this happen? Why can we count on it happening again? Who did this? Water boils at 212 degrees Fahrenheit and freezes at 32. Order, pattern and regularity are part of our lives. On such assumptions scientific enquiry proceeds. Evolution no more explains away God than a car production line explains away a car designer. I am not capable of seeing a plan without belief in a planner, regulation without a regulator, beauty without a source of beauty.

That's a long way from believing in the God of the Christians. Christianity asserts not only that there is an omnipotent God, but also that He or She actually cares for every item of creation and underpins its continual existence. Yet across the whole story of creation lies the shadow and scandal of inexplicable suffering. That's the rub. I can understand the suffering I bring on myself. If I am justly exposed as a hypocrite, or lose a friendship because of some stupid remark or action of mine, I've only myself to blame. But innocent suffering, that's the problem: children in pain, burnt, blown apart. No wonder some people across the centuries – and indeed still now – believe in various sorts of dualism. A good God in a permanent contest with an evil one: light against darkness.

At the end of the day I just accept that there are aspects of suffering that I will never understand. My sense of justice is outraged, yet that passionate sense of justice in itself is a real fact of creation. Where did that come from? Perhaps the ability that I have to judge God is only made possible because of the gifts that I have also been given by God. In Christianity, innocent yet redemptive suffering plays a central part. The Cross was not only an event of 2000 years ago, but continues in the life of the Church of today.

But what about *my* significance? Some people appear to think that if one does not believe in personal immortality then the non-existence of God must follow. That I can't understand. The footprints of God are all over creation. What happens to us individually is a secondary matter. What the fullness of life in an after-life will actually mean I have almost no idea, but I don't believe that, once created, we simply vanish from history. If that were the case there could be no balance of justice and no resolution to the problem of innocent suffering.

Furthermore, though my Christian faith has a solid historical foundation, it involves mystery and misunderstanding. That should be no surprise. The ant that crawls over the face of a computer knows nothing about the power of information just under its little legs. The blind man can only have a sunset explained in words. Our knowledge of what is comes through our limited five senses. Of the richness of reality we have only the vaguest knowledge. When I say that my faith has a historical base it is because I believe in the life and teaching of Jesus Christ, the most amazing and heroic human being who lived and died in a specific place at a specific time.

Our modern understanding of the wide variety of forms of literature in the different books of the Bible does not reduce it to a work of fantasy or fiction. Jesus lived and died at a time and place, and we know a great deal about what He said and did. That His first followers believed that He rose from the tomb and was present to them in different ways is also a matter of historical record.

He is a leader worth following unconditionally. In his 30-odd years He gave the world a new message, and presented an old one in a new way. That message is that the kingdom of God is here, just behind the curtain of our physical world. Those who are citizens of that kingdom are to challenge the norms of contemporary life with a different set of values. Power is an obstacle, money an impediment, national exclusivity absurd, ownership only on trust and temporary, God to be found in the poorest, marginalized and discarded. Enemies are to be loved, forgiven and turned into friends. This is the gospel of non-violence.

Most of the definitions that we have used over the centuries to try to identify and pin Jesus down fail me. God and Man, one person, two natures – but what that actually means is quite beyond me. God does not go into a box of our making. So it is also with the nature of God. On the evidence of things said and done, we believe it makes sense to talk of a Trinity in the Godhead – three persons sharing one nature. But what does that mean? We go back to the ant on the computer.

That's one half of the question. The second comes in another form. If you are a Christian why, considering the way that the Catholic Church behaves so often, are you still a Catholic? Well why not? I was born and baptized into the Catholic Church. I have lived my life in that part of the Christian world. I have loyalties and loves in that faith community. What would make me want to move? Corruption? But corruption is a normal feature of human institutions, even of Churches and other institutions that hold up ideals which they fail to achieve.

So it has been from the days of the Acts of the Apostles onwards. Fraud gets its first mention in chapter 5. This does not for one minute mean tolerating the abuse of power, financial corruption or dishonesty in any form. The renewal of the Church has been an ongoing process century after century, and so it will be long into the future.

One of my favourite hymns expresses so well the notion that personally and collectively we do not always achieve what we want to achieve but that everything can be redeemed:

> Take all that daily toil plants in our heart's
> poor soil,
> Take all we start and spoil, each hopeful
> dream,
> The chances we have missed, the graces we
> resist,
> Lord, in the Eucharist, take and redeem.

(Kevin Nichols, 'In Bread We Bring You, Lord')

But in any event, even if my church were as awful as some critics suppose, where is one meant to go? That God is known and honoured in non-Christian religions is quite clear, but those roads are not mine, though I have many friends who travel on them. So too I have many friends amongst the Quakers, the Anglicans, the Methodists and the Orthodox. Each of those communities has their own very valuable and impressive spiritual features. But they too are human institutions. They too have their corporate failings. The grass is always greener somewhere else. I have ended up in one field and in that field I propose to stay.

Let me now be more positive. I am not just a Catholic because I can't think of anywhere else to go. I am a Catholic because in that community I meet so many wonderful men and women, now and of the past, who have travelled the same road towards God. The Catholic Church is, on the whole, a classless and international community. I know I am meant to be wrapped up in piety after receiving Communion at mass on a Sunday, but instead I often look at the rag-tag procession going up with me to take their part in the Lord's Supper of today. New babies get carried up for a blessing; old people come with the lines of life across their faces; refugees struggle to understand our English; and those in wheelchairs are pushed up to the altar by their friends. Community life in a parish does much to help burst the bubble of self-importance. I am just one amongst many on the journey of life inspired by the vision of hope and centuries of faith.

Prayer? Well I'm all for prayer, even though I can't keep my mind on anything for more than ten seconds without finding that it has got free and galloped off into the distance. Prayer, however, is more than the art of concentration. I call it cleaning the windows of my life. In other words, letting the light of God and His values shine inside me. 'For thine is the kingdom, the power and the glory . . .' – the complete ending of the Lord's Prayer has become something of a mantra. I say it on the Tube, when queuing at the post office and even when that metallic voice tells me, as I wait endlessly on the phone, 'your call is important to us . . .'. My mantra does more to reduce my blood pressure than does my Amlodipine.

At the same time, the life of prayer and sacraments telescopes time, lifts the veil and brings the eternal just within reach. If most of life is looking at shadows from the eternal on the wall, the sacraments take us through to life everlasting. They are little windows through which we move to that ultimate reality hidden behind bread and wine, and our varied fellow parishioners.

So my current local community does much to keep me a Catholic. What goes on in Rome is sometimes a pleasure but more frequently an annoyance. Ronald Knox is meant to have said that he didn't mind being on the barque of Peter but he hoped he would never have to get near the engine-room.

It is not only the local community of Catholic Christians that keeps me in the fold. It is also my membership, now 40 years old, of the peace and justice movement Pax Christi, where I find a fellowship of faith and action. After all, the Church is not just about personal salvation or even charitable works, but also about radical global transformation. My Church teaches 'the gospel is there not just to free us from sin but from what sin has done to our society'. In Pax Christi I find a sustaining sense of purpose, mission and enthusiasm for the practical work of that transformation. It has become a central part of my Christian life. It brings together two aspects of faith often kept apart: prayer and politics. The two go hand in hand.

The Catholic Church has been my home for all of 70 plus years. I have learned to respect other families of faith in a way that I did not in the past. I have ceased to try to count converts as if one was notching up cricket scores in the way that we once did. We Catholics are now paying a heavy price for our hubris in Britain in the 1950s and 1960s. All Christian Churches are now under challenge on a wide variety of issues. In the world of the typical *Guardian* feature writer we are the obscurants who not only continue to cherish ancient myths, but whose myths actually impede the progress of humanity. No good mentioning that the worst horrors of the twentieth century were not those of the Church but the responsibility of Hitler, Stalin, Mussolini and Pol Pot.

Of course, the failings of the Church upset and sometimes anger me. Greed, power, lust, cruelty and cowardice: they're all there in the history of the Church. But that's only part of the story and not the major part for me. The

Church connects me to people across both geography and history: bright lights who have pursued a different vision of a different world. I feel both pride and admiration when, while the TV camera is bringing us disaster shots from faraway lands, it often enough falls on some priest, nun or lay worker. Such people, miles away from their home countries, have been hard at the work of teaching, nursing, praying, promoting economic solidarity and defending human rights wherever people are suffering in the world – often at a price. There are as many heroes and martyrs today as there were in days gone by.

Two contemporary figures have particularly influenced me. One is Dorothy Day. New York communist and convert to a radical but traditional Catholicism, she was the inspiration behind the Catholic Worker movement which, in my mind, represents Christianity at its best. Alongside her stands Franz Jagerstatter, the Austrian farmer who, almost alone against the tide of opinion of his day, refused to submit to the Caesar of Nazi Germany and was beheaded as a consequence.

There are, of course, many other twentieth-century names to be honoured and everyone will have their own list. Mine includes Archbishops Helder Camara and Oscar Romero, Barbara Ward and Pope John XXIII. They are part of a long line of Christian witnesses going back even to the martyr Maximilian, who said, when ordered to take the oath and join the Roman army in 295 AD: 'I am not a soldier of this world but a soldier of God.'[1] They encourage me today. St Francis of Assisi, apostle of peace, St Peter Damien, brother of lepers, St Teresa of Avila, critic of popes, and Julian of Norwich are all inspirations. To friends bereaved I always send that little message from Julian: 'From Him we come, in Him we are enfolded, to Him we return.'

No history of humanity would be complete without an acknowledgement of the part played by the whole Christian world in giving us hospitals and alms houses, schools and universities. The preservation of civilization at a dark time and the development of agriculture owe much to the monastic orders. Christian culture has contributed enormously to art, music and architecture. The witness of the silent, prayerful orders is a permanent encouragement to all of us in the hurly-burly of daily life.

My Church is an extraordinary institution and includes within it almost every shade of opinion. Brian Frost, author and poet, has said that there are 'many faces to the Catholic Church, the longest surviving multi-racial, multi-cultural organization history has known'.

It is not the sins but the lack of vision that upsets me. Too often the Church here looks like a beleaguered fortress of the increasingly elderly faithful, terrified of a world outside and endlessly respectful of whoever happens to have political power. We are meant to be a light to the Gentiles, citizens of another universal kingdom. Professor Philip Allott of Cambridge University recently had this to say:

> Catholic Christianity should be a triumphant affirmation of a dimension of human life for which Western civilization now makes no provision. It fills the faithful with a justified self-confidence and a spontaneous generosity, and an exceptional sense of social responsibility that can come only from living within a universal and perennial transcendental perspective which makes them into a different kind of human being.[2]

Yet too often we have become a community which has absorbed and not challenged contemporary norms. From

43

unjustly differentiated salary scales to 7-day 24-hour shopping, from education judged by its commercial advantage to military solutions for international problems, we have adapted exactly where we should have challenged. And where we do challenge – as we do – over the 180,000 abortions every year in the UK alone, do we give the right answers? I do not believe that recriminalization of all abortions is the only acceptable Christian response to this slaughter. Still less do I believe it to be the only moral issue on which to judge politicians.

In this country, as in Rome, the centralization of the Church has proceeded apace and its clericalism remains as strong as ever. The organizations which, in the early days after the Second Vatican Council, made possible lay participation in decision making have either never sprouted or have withered away. We remain immature children in our Church community, while we preach participatory democracy to the rest of the world. To meet the immediate crisis of the diminishing number of clergy and religious in this part of the world, an army of salaried lay administrators are now in place – good people, I do not doubt, but co-opted into the existing system rather than a challenge to it.

Enough of moaning. Change in the Church will come and has come. In the 1980s nuclear deterrence was given a conditional blessing. Now the papal representative at the United Nations calls it 'an obstacle to peace'. Church strictures on the environmental and developmental damage done by modern global capitalism and its free market, muted during the Cold War, have become frequent and powerful. No one spoke more regularly or more firmly against recent wars, and especially against the disastrous American invasion of Iraq, than Pope John Paul II.

Hope springs eternal. I have in front of me an excellent report on penal reform, produced at the end of 2004 by the

Catholic Bishops' Conference of England and Wales.[3] It is bolder and more imaginative than anything I have seen elsewhere. New ideas are there also at local level. Despite the isolationist and racist language of so much of the popular media and of too many politicians, Church responses to the refugee and asylum-seeker crisis have been so encouraging.

Other Catholics will have their own reasons for hope. Flowers pop up in the garden, sometimes where we least expect them. When I am discouraged about Catholicism in the Western world my heart suddenly lifts when I learn about the courage, vigour and growth of Catholic communities in faraway places from the Philippines to Central America.

Why am I still a Catholic? Because through the Catholic Church I am reminded on a weekly basis that God exists, that I can be united with Him and that He has spoken to us in words, works and wonders. More than that because I, a speck of dust amongst the aeons and galaxies, here today and gone tomorrow, am a person of value with my own talents and part to play in building the Kingdom of God. I see no reason whatever to leave the Church, but plenty of reason for wanting it to be reformed and renewed.

NOTES

1. Paul Burns, *Butler's Lives of Saints* (London: Continuum, 2003).
2. Philip Allott. *The Tablet*, 11 December 2004.
3. Catholic Bishops' Conference of England and Wales, *A Place of Redemption* (London: Continuum, 2004).

On the Sidelines of a Culture of Death

Neil Scolding, 46, has been Burden Professor of Clinical Neurosciences, and Consultant in Neurology, at the University of Bristol and Frenchay Hospital since 1999. His particular research and clinical interest is in stem cell repair in Multiple Sclerosis using adult-derived stem cells. He has been Chairman of the Board of Governors of the Linacre Centre for Health Care Ethics since 2002.

In December 2000 public discussion in Britain about human cloning and stem cells was at its modest height. Parliament was debating the issue and the 'Cloning Bill' was about to be passed. I was invited to the House of Commons to contribute to a briefing meeting for MPs. I was to talk on 'The Potential of Adult Stem Cells in Neurological Disease'.

It was my first visit to Westminster. I was to be the first speaker at the briefing session. I had long been concerned that the enormous scientific progress concerning adult stem cells (stem cells taken from living adults as opposed to those derived from specially created embryos) and their potential for developing therapies had gone virtually unreported in the popular press, which had focused almost entirely on the debate around using the embryos in this way. So I was delighted to have the privileged opportunity to educate our legislators. Fools rush ...

Jenny Tonge, Liberal Democrat MP and meeting chairperson, briefly introduced me. Her last, extraordinary sentence was (something like) 'I should say that I will ask all the speakers, before they talk, to declare their religious or faith background.' Taken aback but unprotesting, grasping wildly and in vain for an articulate response explaining why this was an outrageous request, I lamely acceded. 'My name is Neil and I am a Catholic.'

There was a barely inaudible sigh of relief from the great majority of the audience who, having arrived with a pre-determined and immovable conviction supporting destructive embryonic stem cell research, deeply appreciated the perfect excuse they'd now been given to ignore all I might say about the viable alternative of using stem cells from living adults. After all, no Catholic could be remotely trusted to speak a scientific truth on any subject relating to human embryos. Annihilation!

Everything I said thereafter about the successful isolation of adult stem cells, their proliferative capacity, their multipotentiality, animal studies showing their regenerative and reparative abilities in different disease models, and the ease and speed of translating bone marrow stem cell research from laboratory to clinical practice had been fatally torpedoed in the perception of the audience. He'd have to say all that, I could see them thinking. He's a Catholic.

A few months later, my failure to influence my audience was made more evident when the relevant bill was duly passed, making the UK the only country in the world at that time to legalize the cloning of human embryos with no purpose other than to use them as a source of stem cells. (In America, for example, it was not illegal as such, but no government funding was or is permitted for it, effectively stopping it.)

So, why as a scientist and after experiences like this, am I still a Catholic? First and probably foremost, I am a Catholic because I have chosen to be. So, in most regards is every other Catholic, of course, but I am a convert, having had a mildly Anglican upbringing, then becoming slightly more stringently Anglican – and a confirmand – in my twenties, only to be received into the Catholic Church a few years later.

This is not just relevant, but in many ways the key to all I could say. To an individual who deliberated (however superficially) and chose to become a Catholic, the extraordinarily commonly encountered assumption that (in relation to stem cells, embryos and the like) no one need listen for a moment to one's views because, essentially, they are not one's own, is particularly frustrating. 'He's just parroting the usual party line.'

One of the main reasons I *became* a Catholic was the clear attitude to life that the Church of Rome holds: a Church that neither proclaimed nor really held a clear respect for human life is not a happy one. As Cardinal Newman has said: 'We can believe what we choose. We are answerable for what we choose to believe.'[1]

It must be said that there were other less lofty and, then, no less prominent reasons for converting. It was at the time when I began to take my small children to church. Our Anglican church was, perhaps atypically, not child-friendly, and the opprobrium directed towards the slightest paediatric disturbance was a very effective invitation to seek alternative accommodation. Perhaps this is unfair – many other Anglican churches may have been completely different – but it played an important role. The infinitely more relaxed, even indulgent (of infants) atmosphere in Catholic churches was compelling.

These two catalysts – respect for pre-natal life, encouragement of post-natal – are not small details, and they are related. The easy welcoming (not tolerance) of young families, with the mild disruption they bring, reflects a fundamentally different, healthier and more wholesome approach to the Church. The mass, and so Catholicism itself, is not a performance, not an add-on. It is part of normal life and is all the more, not less, important for this.

But this same belief in itself, its confidence in the normalness of faith, protects Catholicism from the constant self-doubt, permanent questioning and inevitable compromise that mark contemporary Anglicanism. Of course, this applies not just to the subject of stem cells and embryos: almost everything appears negotiable.

So I left behind a powerful combination of high doctrinal woolliness with on-the-ground formality. Not that the decision was easy for me. A streak of *laissez-faire* idleness, dressed up as a traditionalist distaste for change, certainly held me back. The Church of England is after all so *English*, and the Church of Rome seemed so foreign. Others have written of the sense of lacking patriotism felt in 'going over'. Substituting the prose and poise of the *Book of Common Prayer* and the *King James Bible* for the often-painful Catholic equivalents was a wrench. And likewise leaving behind the peaceful solidity of ancient English churches seemed no less than a small tragedy.

But the country churches I so loved were, after all, Catholic in origin. And in any case these are all accidents rather than substance. They did not, and I thought could not, measure against 'the heir and image of the primitive

Church'. It was also helpful to recall that far better and more philosophically minded men than I – and certainly not inferior lovers of Englishness – Newman and Chesterton – had, doubtless with a better grasp of the fundamentals than I, found it imperative to jump.

The *earthiness* of Catholics also appealed (as it did to them). Yes, the Roman Church has its ascetic, self-denying tradition, but it also embraces an 'eat, drink and be merry' wing. 'Catholic men that live upon wine/Are deep in the water, and frank, and fine.'[2] Who could fail to feel at home with, say, Compton Mackenzie's Father Macalister as he settles down to read Wild West thrillers, asks after Celtic's football results and above all hopes his guests might join him in a 'small sensation'? (And of whom in *Whisky Galore* [the English] Mr Brown opines: 'A most eccentric sort of person. He's not at all my idea of a priest.')

I think it would also be a mistake to see such behaviour as merely a happy eccentricity or oddity. It is much more than that. It is surely rather the consequence of a sheer solidity of faith. The hearty churchman, comfortably celebrating the 'trinity of eating, drinking and praying', bears splendid witness to a vital and exuberant Catholicism partly because he shows to the world a fulsome love of his (or her) God-given life – which is no distance at all from loving, respecting and protecting others' lives.

Chesterton's 'trinity' perfectly captures the naturalness of prayer that can only reflect a real, unaffected belief. Newman noted that Catholics are 'easy and cheerful in their mention of sacred things,'[3] and this fundamental ease surely translates to an enjoyment of life, and its pleasures.

So why *still* a Catholic? It's certainly the case that, as a clinical neuroscientist interested in developing therapies with an aim to bring about the repair of the diseased or damaged brain or spinal cord, my professional life might have been easier had I been other than a Catholic. Doubtless, my inflexibility has brought certain difficulties.

Having a scientific talk rubbished – whether in a Commons' committee room or in a more conventional debate elsewhere – because of my 'faith background' is painful. On the other hand, the privilege and pleasure of being asked to do such things cannot be overlooked, and indirectly has related origins.

More generally, the accusation of being Luddite, and callous, in 'denying current and future generations of sufferers cures of their diseases' through opposing human embryonic stem cell research is both tiresome and occasionally (depending on the source) distressing. Being both labelled and dismissed as a member of an off-message community of recusant scientists and other assorted fundamentalists, fanatics and ne'er-do-wells can be a mild annoyance. The perpetual sense of being seriously out of kilter with my peers is a strain.

Whether it has more significantly affected my research or professional success or otherwise is difficult to judge objectively. The major grant-giving bodies in the UK, both government and charitably funded, have made their position very clear regarding the propriety of continuing destructive human embryo research, including human cloning for embryonic stem cells. It must, they say, without reservation, be facilitated. Moreover, the community of grant body scientists and research peers who advise these bodies is extremely small and fairly intimate, so I certainly feel anxious about publicly declaring and adhering to a position which is directly contrary to theirs. Defending that position with arguments which, of necessity, may directly contradict assertions these bodies have made can hardly engender feelings of great affection on their part.

So what is this clash of science and ethics really about?

Those of us interested in the enormously exciting and promising field of clinical science that has become known as 'regenerative medicine' will need large numbers of cells. We need them to replace and repair damaged tissues. Neurologists like myself will need specialized brain cells – of many, many different types – to repair brain damage, whatever the cause of that damage, be it stroke, trauma, Multiple Sclerosis, Parkinson's Disease, Alzheimer's or Motor Neurone Disease. Cardiologists need cells that will repair the heart. Endocrinologists need cells that will yield pancreatic islet cells (that make insulin). Ophthalmologists need a source of retinal cells. And so on. Each of us will need large numbers of them: millions, and more likely tens if not hundreds of millions, will be required for each patient to be treated.

Given these needs, it is easy to understand how the possibility of a cell source which (a) can turn into any of the specialized cell types required, and (b) can divide in an effectively unlimited way, thereby potentially generating virtually infinite numbers of cells, is received with huge (but sadly not very critical) enthusiasm. 'Embryonic stem cells (are) … the Holy Grail in finding a cure for cancer, Parkinson's Disease, diabetes, osteoporosis, Alzheimer's and Multiple Sclerosis,' Yvette Cooper, the health minister told *The Times* on 16 December 2000. These requirements are in essence the defining properties of the stem cell – the 'stem' of all types of tissue, these can indeed turn into all of the different cell types needed and, by having the capacity to self-renew, can yield unlimited numbers.

The problem, of course, is that the obvious place to look for such cells is where, intuitively, cells with these properties must logically be found. During the nine months it takes for a fertilized egg – a single cell – to develop into the delivered infant, it is self-evident that cells with these properties must emerge and contribute to that growth and development. So it was that stem cells were first found in embryonic tissue.

So far, not so bad, since in the long-standing tradition of biological and medical science, it was in the rodent embryo that these experiments were carried out. (By no means a simple ethical issue in itself, but not one to be addressed here.) But for developing treatments for human disease, human stem cells must of course be studied. And so, the argument ran, human embryos must be utilized as the source of stem cells. Since embryonic stem cells cannot be isolated from the embryo without destroying it, the stage is set for diametrically opposed positions to emerge – zealots (yes, we've had that one too) on the one hand, determined to prevent this research and so condemn millions of unfortunates needlessly to suffer, versus enlightened, compassionate, etc., etc., scientists on the other.

The difficulty lies in how we perceive the human embryo. For advocates of destructive human embryonic stem cell research, the human embryo is certainly 'due special status, and special respect'[4] (terminology offered by Baroness Mary Warnock, of whom more anon), but the real question is 'when does the developing foetus acquire the moral status of a live human?'

In presenting the question in this way, there is, of course, an implicit assertion that there is a stage when the foetus does not enjoy this privilege. A gradation therefore emerges, and it becomes a simple issue of balance, to be solved by any enlightened intellect's set of scales – after all, 'special' is a wholly subjective, comparative and qualitative attribute. So an equation must be drawn: when is the growing moral status of a foetus sufficiently weighty to match the potential benefit to humankind of the therapies to be developed from its own cells? After this time, destructive research is bad, before it, good.

This doesn't hold water for the rest of us. 'When does the developing foetus acquire the moral status of a live human?' is a non-question, the answer being so self-evident. It must do so when it becomes a live human, and it is a live human from its very beginning. For what is it if not living from the moment of conception? What is it if not human?

Considering it is we who are dismissed as the emotionally driven, anti-science Luddites, it is extraordinary that the word 'human' is so loosely and non-scientifically used by those in favour of destructive embryo research. 'Human' is a species, and the embryo of which we speak is at any time in its development a member of no other. The assertion that Catholics, or pro-lifers of other faiths or none, are also Luddite and anti-science in concerning themselves about what is no more than a 'ball of cells' is similarly extraordinary: we are all no more than 'balls of cells'. The implication that only humans who look like small adults need be considered 'human' is, rather, arguably the non-scientific approach. Moral status cannot depend on size.

The tiniest conceptus is a human being: it is human; it exists, has being – this surely cannot be remotely contentious. And because it is a human being, it has moral status: it cannot be simply destroyed, whatever might be the benefit for humankind, any more than any other member of the human species can be experimented upon merely 'for the wider benefit'.

This principle, formerly considered self-evident, first required a more explicit enunciation after the Second World War. The *Nuremberg Code* of 1947 (emerging from the Nuremberg Trials) declared 'experiments performed on an individual must be of benefit to the individual, not just benefit society,' and the 'individual' concerned was explicitly defined as human life from the time of conception.

This precept was directly incorporated into the later *Declaration of Helsinki* (1964), a universally accepted statement of basic medical and bio-ethics. We do not experiment on a fellow human, unless potentially for that human's own benefit.

Note that this is based on the 'human-ness' of the foetus, obviously present from conception. That the tiniest foetus is a human being, and deserves to be treated as such, does not depend on or imply that it is necessarily a person. 'Personhood' is altogether more difficult to define, scientifically ambiguous and subjective, open to (and we might say requiring) a religious dimension – ensoulment, animation and so on. Whilst this is important, and does help to explain the 'ball of cells' position – I too would find it difficult to consider, say, a cluster of two cells a *person* – it is not fundamental to the position I have put forward. To consider a human a person is an act of the subject, and necessarily subjective, and an unsafe basis therefore for deciding matters of life and death of the 'object' at hand.

What is a constant source of surprise to me is not just that informed and thoughtful clinicians and biologists can disagree, but that they do so with such confidence. Many God-fearing Christians have applied the best of their intellect, biological knowledge and wisdom to these questions, and have, honestly and with good intent, appeared to conclude that the human embryo is not a human being, or is disposable for the greater good. But do they never doubt themselves? Surely they must? Surely they do not consider themselves infallible?

How do they ignore the fact that if, small chance though they might allow it, their careful and occasionally eruditely described position should, in the ultimate analysis, prove wrong, they would have advocated, argued for, risked complicity in, the deliberate killing of humans? What could be more serious? As Orwell has said: 'When people really believed in Hell, they were not so fond of striking graceful attitudes on its brink.'[5]

That there is an alternative source of stem cells is then a valuable bonus in making one's arguments – but in fact probably shouldn't be so described: there is always an alternative in medicine and science. We now know that in most adult tissues there are small numbers of cells with stem cell properties rendering them useful for developing therapies. At present, bone marrow stem cells appear to have most potential, but other adult tissue sources may in future years be seen to hold advantages over these. These cells can be isolated, expanded to produce enormous numbers and can turn into all of the cell types we might reasonably require for regenerative therapies.

They have additional biological advantages: we have used bone marrow cells for decades in different forms of therapies (for leukaemias and other blood disorders), so we know well how to obtain, store and use marrow cells effectively. Moreover, we now know that the huge numbers of patients who have received bone marrow transplants for such haematological disorders will have 'inadvertently' received small numbers of these stem cells. Indeed the finding that donor, bone-marrow-derived cells can be seen years later to have turned into highly specialized and functioning brain cells and other cell types in the recipients helps unequivocally to confirm their capacity for differentiating – and all this with no ill effect, helping to prove their safety.

Also, since cells would be taken from the marrow of the patient (with, say, Parkinson's Disease) to be treated, they would not be seen as 'foreign tissue' by the recipient and so not be rejected – another serious problem with embryonic cells.

Besides all of which, we now understand that it is the normal function of these bone-marrow-derived stem cells to circulate, enter damaged tissues and contribute to local repair, much as the function of immune cells is to circulate, enter areas of infection and fight the microbe. The body's repair system can, of course, be overwhelmed, leading to explicit disease, just as the immune system is overwhelmed in symptomatic infection. But supplementing and augmenting the repair system using greater numbers of stem cells (collected, expanded in the laboratory and perhaps also turned into the specific, required cell type before re-injection) is likely to increase its efficacy, just as supplementing the immune system artificially (by active and passive immunization, for example) works as a treatment.

By contrast, the 'normal' function of the embryonic stem cell is to form an embryo and then a foetus, not to repair diseased adult tissues: placing these cells into the latter is to confront them with a wholly alien environment and expect of them a wholly unnatural task. The biological reasons for expecting success of adult marrow stem cells in disease states seem to me far more persuasive.

All these advantages have meant that bone marrow stem cells are already being used for their regenerative potential, in stark contrast to embryonic stem cells (even for those derived from sources other than cloning), which again the most ardent advocates recognize are a decade or more from being used in patients. Preliminary and more complicated (placebo-controlled) trials have now shown the benefit (in cardiac recovery) of injecting adult, bone-marrow-derived stem cells into the hearts of victims of heart attacks. Other trials testing the reparative efficacy of these cells in other disorders are well underway.

And, should it need saying, bone marrow cells can be

obtained readily, causing the donor slight discomfort but no harm.

Given all these advantages and advances, I'd have to say I find it very difficult indeed to understand why the arguments continue and why embryonic stem cell research continues to excite enormous excitement and to expand almost exponentially. Much has been invested by proponents, not just financially but scientifically, politically and indeed emotionally. Also scientists, like artists, journalists and mountaineers, simply hate being told there are areas where they may not go, and they react vigorously. I'd have to add that at a detached, dispassionate level, there is that about the embryonic stem cell which is intrinsically more exciting, tantalizing, seductive – sexy, in the common parlance – compared to which adult marrow cells, easily available, and about which we really should have known more decades ago, seem drab and mundane. Scientists are no less prone than ordinary mortals to being irresistibly drawn to topics or technologies which are new and exciting: tortoise versus hare, or Concorde versus 747.

Whatever. But the controversy does still continue, and opprobrium is still distributed liberally in the direction of those who not only do not follow but also articulate opposition to the received establishment position.

So, yes, my position has brought certain difficulties, but 'ten thousand difficulties do not make one doubt'.[6] I'd hope that the foregoing would make it obvious that there's no rational reason whatsoever to consider altering my position, still less my Church. Whether I were to remain a Catholic or not would hardly have great impact on the 'question' of whether a human embryo is human. All human life deserves protection. I believe this, and the Catholic Church so believes and teaches.

It may have been expedient to behave otherwise – grants

might arguably have been easier to come by, one or two slings and arrows dodged (surely only to be struck by others though), and many conversations could have been less uncomfortable for all concerned. Perhaps, then, I remain a Catholic because I know there are certain truths that really cannot be avoided.

Cardinal Cormac Murphy-O'Connor has written:

if we order our hearts and minds to be open to [God's] truth, then nothing is ever quite the same. We can never say, for example, that truth is relative: that everything is merely a matter of choice; nor that the individual, uprooted from any objective reality, should decide for himself or herself what is good and what is evil. Such a view leaves those who cannot exercise freedom of choice very vulnerable. It leaves the unborn child at the mercy of the scalpel, and deprives the elderly and confused of the tubes that will bring them food and water. Who will speak for the weak, when the strong are free to choose?[7]

One does not need to look hard for examples of where the rationalist, relativist approach can lead individuals of even the most admired intellect. Baroness Warnock, who coined the 'special status, special respect' view of embryos, has recently acknowledged 'I am not ashamed to say some lives are more worth living than others.'[8] The Reverend Professor Sir John Polkinghorne, who chaired the government committee looking into experiments using human embryos, reassuringly took the view that 'the live foetus, whether *in utero* or *ex utero* ... should be treated on principles broadly similar to those which apply to ... adults and children,' and yet found himself able to sanction such research and to write, '*with the exception of abortion* ... intervention on a living foetus ... should carry only minimal risk of harm' (my italics).[9]

In the 1980s, when Pope John Paul II first warned of a 'culture of death' in the developed world, it was thought by many to be an over-reaction at best, at worst a slightly counter-productive exaggeration which, because so easy to scoff at and caricature, was meat and drink to the 'opposition'. Events since have confirmed its sad and awful prescience.

So in the end I cannot pretend that still being a Catholic is a matter of consciously and purposefully donning a sword and shield as a 'life warrior', selflessly defending the meek and the mild and the voiceless. In the end it is about merely trying to be honest, and for all one's other faults, trying to avoid at least in this instance ducking what I believe to be true. It is therefore not least a question of searching for peace of mind and, with God's help, seeking and adhering to His truth.

NOTES

1. Cardinal Newman. Letter to Mrs William Froude 27 June 1848, in CS Dessain (ed.), *Letters and Diaries of John Henry Newman*, vol. 12 (Oxford, 1962).
2. Hilaire Belloc.
3. Cardinal Newman, *Apologia Pro Vita Sua* (1864).
4. Baroness Mary Warnock chaired the government committee of inquiry into human fertilization 1982–84.
5. George Orwell (1903–50).
6. Cardinal Newman. *Apologia Pro Vita Sua*. 1864.
7. Cardinal Cormac Murphy-O'Connor.
8. Baroness Mary Warnock.
9. Professor Sir John Polkinghorne. 'Review of the Guidance on the Research Use of Fetuses and Fetal Material'. London: HMSO. 1989.

Angels and Dirt

Peter Stanford, 43, is a writer and broadcaster. He was editor of the Catholic Herald *for four years. His books include biographies of Lord Longford and the Devil and a history of Heaven. He lives in London with his wife and two children.*

I met my wife Siobhan on a blind date. Not on *Blind Date*, though at the time it felt just about as public. We had been fixed up by two recently married friends who watched our every initial move, like pundits in a TV studio scrutinizing a football match. He had known me since college and she worked with Siobhan in the law. The reason they were just convinced we would get on, they told us when we did, was because we were both Catholic. We laughed and thought how foolish of them. Hadn't both of us spent many years refusing to be propelled emotionally in the direction of 'nice Catholic boys and girls' by our parents?

We were the only two Catholics that our matchmakers knew between them. So it was less instinct than necessity that inspired them. Necessity because they were both Jewish, had found each other because they wanted a Jewish spouse, and therefore both possessed a particular take on the role of faith in putting together couples which, in theory, neither Siobhan nor I subscribed to.

So we met. We fell in love. And ten months later we married – in a Catholic church. I can't quite remember how long it took us to admit that being Catholic was part of why it worked between us. It was certainly before the wedding. You want to know what the person you love was like before you met them, how they were raised, about their family, the first record they bought, their fashion horrors. And at every turn as we explored, as every couple does, the prequel to that first meeting, we discovered a remarkable similarity between our experiences (if not our record collections). Her convent grammar school in Norwich paralleled my Christian Brothers grammar school in Birkenhead. Both of us had grown up in a narrow circle of other Catholic families where no one's parents divorced, everybody waited until they were married and things like homosexuality only happened on TV in *Are You Being Served?*

I'd clocked up a few more retreats than Siobhan. While she sensibly preferred Catholic guide camp and the church choir for her extra-curricular activities, I got led astray by a charismatic Christian Brother who was also Charismatic. In a basement room under the Brothers' house, which we named Jerusalem, we'd strum our guitars, wave our hands in the air and pin up cheesy poems to God based on John Denver's 'Annie's Song'.

Naturally and inevitably, both of us had reacted against such constrained and, by the standards of our fellow students, peculiar upbringings when we got to university. I took what I always thought of as a leave of absence rather than my cards, but my sabbatical from church-going was cut short when I landed my first post-graduate job – as the trainee reporter at the Catholic weekly, the *Tablet*. I got it because I was Catholic, had dabbled in a bit of student journalism and because at the interview I vastly overestimated my skills as an Italian speaker and therefore as one capable of translating for the editor the *Osservatore Romano*, the Vatican daily. The vocabulary I had developed lounging around on Elban beaches and ordering in restaurants didn't crop up very much in papal addresses.

It was all an accident, or fate, or God's plan. I'll plump for the second. The third sounds too much like suggesting I'm special. What it certainly wasn't was a vocation, though the pay presupposed I had other motives in taking the job than financial gain. Yet once there, at my manual typewriter in a drafty corridor outside the editor's office, I quickly got hooked on the Church, rather as I might have got hooked on classical music if I'd joined as the junior hack on the *Gramophone*.

But it went deeper. The Church, I came to see, was about the world. It may be a traditionalist institution in its organization, but the gospel, as it interpreted it, was a radical, social one and so it had something to say about every contemporary dilemma in a comprehensive way that classical music lacks. Faith and life connected, and a lot of the time I found what the Catholic Church had to say sounded pretty right. So in the world's political disputes, it tended to be on the side of those I perceived as the goodies. And in its economic and social conflicts, it sided with the marginalized, the needy, those without a voice. Often at great personal cost.

There were the martyrs whose deaths made international headlines, the Oscar Romeros whose faith and courage swept me up. But somehow more pertinent were the Church figures whose deaths for the cause of what was right hardly merited a mention in the global media. Like Father Stanley Rother, whose murder in Guatemala in 1981 was one of the first I wrote about in the *Tablet* and whose example stays with me to this day.

An American priest, he lived amongst and ministered to the people of Santiago Atitlan as they were brutalized by a military dictatorship linked with US Protestant evangelical churches and its death squads. He was warned many times that if he did not leave, he would be killed as other Catholic priests and catechists had been. In simple letters home to his family, Father Stan explained why he was staying put with his adopted people. 'The shepherd cannot run at the first sign of danger. Pray for us that we may be a sign of the love of Christ for our people, that our presence among them will fortify them to endure these sufferings in preparation for the coming of the Kingdom.'[1] On 28 July 1981 three masked men broke into his presbytery at midnight and shot him through the head three times.

It was his Catholic faith that took him to Guatemala, his Catholic faith that kept him there, and his Catholic faith that enabled him to put others before himself even up to his death. Such witness bound me ever closer to Catholicism. One of Pope John Paul II's favourite phrases was that the Church should be a sign of contradiction in a modern, secular, consumerist and self-seeking world. Other Christian churches may be more accommodating, and those accommodations can make them more instantly appealing, but in Catholicism the traditional and the radical mix to extraordinary effect. Stanley Rother, holder of the ancient, hierarchical, unaccountable office of priest, used it to contradict everything Western societies hold dear. Or at least those values of self-protection and timidity in the face of big, complex questions that I may have, but which I despise in myself.

It wasn't all positive. There were (and remain) Catholic teachings that I had little time for – the Church's negative obsession with sexual mechanics for instance – but as I read and reread the gospel, I couldn't fail to notice that Jesus had no interest at all in such matters. We are, He taught, as God made us.

As well as providing a crash course in theology, pastoral practice and the role of the Church in fighting to the death for many a worthwhile cause around the globe, what I was learning each day on the job also touched on more profound issues of identity, the Liverpool-Irish culture in which I had been raised and my instinctive political, social and emotional reaction to the world around me. My points of reference, I started to realize, were all Catholic. What began as a professional interest in the Church of my upbringing was becoming intensely personal.

I moved on from the *Tablet* to the *Catholic Herald* and again fate intervened. The benign elderly editor, Terence Sheehy, was nearing retirement and groomed me as his successor. Eventually I succeeded him and became that rare and exotic creature, a practising Catholic in my twenties.

I remember turning up once in my official capacity to present the prizes at a posh convent boarding school, and walking up to a group of nuns waiting on the front doorstep. 'Hello', I said. 'I wonder if you could help me?' 'I'm sorry, we're a little busy', came back the slightly sharp reply as the sister in question peered inscrutably over my shoulder. 'We're waiting for the editor of the *Catholic Herald*.'

At least Siobhan's mother and her sisters, all raised in Ireland and very close to the Church, were impressed when she told them what I did – or by that stage had done, having moved on to freelance life, but still based around writing and broadcasting on religion.

Our wedding took place in Saint Etheldreda's in Ely Place, London's oldest and most beautiful Catholic church. One of the perks of my erstwhile job was that it had forced me to sample other parishes than my local one. Saint Etheldreda's, with its medieval crypt, once part of the

Bishop of Ely's London palace in pre-Reformation times, had long exerted a special pull. You could somehow feel the whole of English Catholic history. Not only had people worshipped there since before the Reformation, its nave is lined with statues of the martyrs of the persecution that followed Henry VIII's break with Rome.

And so, as we stood there side-by-side on a chilly February early evening at the high altar, the candlelight illuminating the vast stained-glass window behind us, I knew absolutely – as I have known few other things in my life – that this was where I was meant to be. A big part of that was how I felt about Siobhan. And that our parents were there at or next to the altar sharing it with us along with our closest friends. But somewhere in there too was the fact that this was a Catholic church and only its blessing through the sacrament of marriage could have made this joining of the two of us before God feel right.

There are rare moments in most of our lives when we experience a sense of the transcendent. Somehow the context broadens, the tight focus on the here and now loosens and we catch sight fleetingly of another spiritual dimension, of a God-given logic behind the scenes. The artist Stanley Spencer saw it and recorded it memorably in everyday events in his home village of Cookham. 'Angels and dirt' was how he put it.

I once wandered about Cookham on the Thames in Berkshire trying to see through to that other dimension but, try as I might in the churchyard to picture, as Spencer did, the Resurrection, I remained resolutely in this world. I have also struggled to make the same mental journey in prayer, and have come to the conclusion that I am both naturally impatient and hopeless at letting go.

The nearest I have come to experiencing the transcendent is in liturgy. There is something unique about the

Catholic liturgy that I find manages to carry you somewhere else and which – again just for me – is missing in the
rituals of other faiths. If I analyse each of the components, it
should be possible to reproduce it elsewhere. The music, the
beauty of ancient and modern buildings, the words, the
ineffable concepts that they struggle so poetically to express,
the stillness, the movement, the timelessness, the sense that
at the Eucharist Christ is so close we can reach out and
touch Him. Yet there is something beyond all that – a
mystery that is made palpable but not unravelled in the
process, a group dynamic that manages to remain so very
individual, a link to another level that is felt but never seen.

And so on that day of our wedding, transported for once
from the back row of the pews to the altar, wanting to drink
in every detail, every face around me, every word, every
gesture, I nonetheless also found myself both there and
elsewhere, joined not only to my new wife but also to some
greater pattern that made what we were both promising to do
less a contract or a commitment and more something blessed.

Words somehow seem inadequate, which is a terrible
admission for a writer to make, though having produced a
book about how humankind has seen heaven down the
ages,[2] I have begun to appreciate that some things we aspire
to and believe in are quite beyond description or depiction.

That book showed me there are many ways to God and I
have not a drop of evangelical blood in my veins. I have no
desire to convert anyone to Catholicism and used to tut
(inwardly) when researching my biography of Lord Longford[3] when he would ask me, about a mutual friend, 'any
chance of them coming over?' To Rome, he meant. Perhaps
it was a generational thing.

Catholicism is what inspires me, what brings me close to
God, what makes me a better person than I otherwise would
have been. Others must find their own path.

There are moments when I do feel profoundly ashamed of my Church. The paedophile priest scandal was just one instance. The on-going failure of senior churchmen to realize and acknowledge in public that the gravest damage has been done not to the reputation of the Church, not to the decent members of the priesthood, but rather to innocent children who will carry into adulthood terrible scars shows an appalling blindness and arrogance in the institution. The activities of papally approved organizations like Opus Dei remain a scandal. The ill-treatment of so many of the faithful – whether they be divorcees denied the sacraments because they have found love again, or brave campaigning priests and bishops who risked their lives for their Church but who have been silenced because their views no longer fit with the Vatican's line – is wicked.

And yet. There can be no excuses, but somehow next to the witness of Stanley Rother I have learnt to accept the failures of the institution and still go forward in faith. Recently I was in Angola in a town called Uige (wee-juh). For 30 years it had been a battleground between opposing sides in the civil war there, a conflict drawn out by the intervention of foreign powers. The place was destroyed. There was no electricity, no water, no shelter and precious little hope. I was taken to a hospital where the queues of mothers and fathers with sick children in their arms stretched round and round the building. So desperate were they that the sight of a white face made them step forward and hold out their child to me with an imploring look. The one doctor inside told me that 80 per cent of them would be dead in the morning, victims of malaria, the absence of drugs and the criminal neglect of their government which makes a fortune from its oil reserves, but pockets it to the tune of billions of dollars a year.

This was hell on earth. I have never felt so impotent. I

was in shock and wanted to weep but that would have been self-indulgent. I, after all, would be going back to England in a few days to my comfortable home and my healthy children.

At my side was an extraordinary Brazilian nun who had chosen to live her life among these people and try to help them in their remorseless and utterly unnecessary suffering. 'Why?' I asked her when we finally sat down at the end of a long day. 'How did she find the strength?' 'Because it is what God has called me to do', she told me, 'because of my Catholic faith, because this is what the Jesus of the gospels would have done'. Next to hers, my own Catholic faith is a poor, frail thing, but I know that, however inadequately, I want to share in what she has.

NOTES

1. Henri Nouwen, *Love in a Fearful Land* (1985).
2. Peter Stanford, *Heaven: A Traveller's Guide to the Undiscovered Country* (London: HarperCollins, 2002).
3. Peter Stanford, *Lord Longford: An Authorized Life* (London: Heinemann, 1994).

Thy Will Be Done

Patricia Scotland, 48, joined Tony Blair's government as a Foreign Office Minister in 1999, moving on to be Minister of State in the Home Office. Married with two sons, she was born in Dominica and grew up in east London. A barrister by profession, she was the youngest ever Queen's Counsel when appointed in 1991. Six years later she accepted a life peerage as Baroness Scotland of Asthal.

I was the child of a mixed faith family, the tenth of twelve children. My father was a Methodist and my mother Catholic, so I was baptised a Catholic and brought up ecumenically. The result was that for many years I simply did not appreciate that the difference between the Protestant tradition and Catholicism was important. My parents brought me up to concentrate on what binds the two traditions instead of what separates them. I was a Christian first and a Catholic second.

It was only when I was 20 and had just finished my law degree that I felt I had to decide what exactly I was. To which tradition would I commit. Two of my brothers and one of my sisters had become Anglicans. I started to read the Bible. There were many paths to the Father, it told me. In my Father's house, there are many rooms.

Perhaps I didn't need to tie myself down to a single

approach, but the more I prayed and reflected on it, the more convinced I became that Catholicism was the only thing that was true for me. And I had to have that which I could accept as having the integrity I needed. And carry on needing. It wasn't something that I particularly welcomed. I seem to recall that in fact I was cross that it was Catholicism because I knew it would be harder to live out.

I had been reading and rereading the Sermon on the Mount and the various accounts of the Last Supper. Going back to the Bible was the Methodist part of me. It was what we had done as children with my father. I looked at the Protestant interpretation of 'this is My Body, this is My Blood' and the Sermon on the Mount and what those two seminal parts of His teaching demanded from us. There were lots of things about the Protestant approach which would make life easier, which took the edge off some of the toughest teachings, which were – to my lawyer's mind – get-out clauses.

In particular, I concentrated on His teaching on marriage. No matter which way I read it, it said you could not divorce your spouse. I could see it would be easier if there were circumstances in which this were possible – as the Protestant Churches teach – but that is not what He said. It was uncomfortable but true, though I accept what is true for me is not necessarily what is true for everyone else.

So I chose Catholicism because I thought it was true. That's the purist in me. That's why I'm still a Catholic. For me the host is and always will be His body, and when I take His body and drink His blood He becomes part of and lives in me.

Faith has always been integrated into my everyday life. When I was little it never occurred to me to question it. My mother had been a daily communicant in the Caribbean where I was born. She still says the Angelus every day at six in the morning, midday and six at night. If she's up at midnight, she says it then too. If she's in the middle of cooking, she will just stop. We grew up with faith not being something you put on as a cloak on Sunday. We lived it every day.

My mother's language was peppered by faith. So it was 'we'll do X tomorrow, if God spares us', or 'God willing'. If we had a problem we were told 'just pray about it', or 'offer it up'. If we were facing a problem, she would reassure us 'this too will pass'. And if ever things were really bad, she would say you have to understand that for anyone to hurt you, they have to go through God first. So He was my shield, my protector. Anything was possible if I had faith.

We came to live in Waltham Forest in east London when I was three. It was the late fifties, the time when you could see signs in windows saying 'No Dogs, No Irish, No Blacks'. My mother truly thought she had arrived in hell. There was a Catholic church in the area but it was quite a long walk. We were the only black family in the congregation and I get the distinct impression from my mother that it wasn't quite as welcoming as it might have been.

However, there was a wonderful local Anglo-Catholic vicar who came to visit us. My mother, he said, had all these lovely children and he had this lovely empty church. 'Wouldn't it be lovely', he asked, 'if your children came to Sunday school?' So we did. Although we continued in the Catholic tradition I was, when invited, allowed to go to several different churches as a child. In some churches I really felt His presence and in some I did not. I was comfortable wherever I thought He happened to be. So I was comfortable in a Pentecostal church. I was comfortable in a Methodist church. I was comfortable in a Baptist church. And I was comfortable in the Catholic church.

I had an experience when I was quite young, perhaps six

75

or seven. I had gone with my brothers and sisters to Downes Park in Hackney. It was a large open space where we used to play, but that day there was an evangelical revival meeting going on with people preaching. We stood on the outer circle of this meeting giggling and listening. At one stage, the speaker announced 'anyone who wants to receive Christ, put their hand up'. For a joke I put my hand up. It is a moment in my life that I will never ever forget because as I went forward I did feel the spirit of God. Or at least I felt changed. Afterwards I became really, really quiet. I didn't know what it was at the time but I felt very, very different from any way I had ever felt before.

That presence, what I came in time to see as that real presence I had felt that day, never left me thereafter. When I look back now I can see that I sound quite odd, a curious creature. On another occasion, when I was 13, I had a paper round. It was early in the morning and I was out delivering papers. Something or someone made me frightened. I wanted to run home. As I'd been taught, I immediately started to pray that God would help me and get me through this. I asked Him to come to my rescue. The air was very still, and then out of nowhere there was this wind. I felt Him in the wind. Again it sounds weird, but I remember it as clearly as anything.

Throughout my life there have been occasions when I have prayed hard about something or for someone and I have then seen that which I have prayed for come into being. So for me there can be no question about faith in God. It is not that someone has told me to believe. Rather there have been so many things in my life that make me believe. I feel very fortunate. Those who haven't had such experiences and yet believe are the ones who are truly extraordinary. It would be very difficult for me not to have faith.

I'm making myself sound as if I was a very strange 20-year-old. I was somebody who loved people, who was joyous about life, who had loads of friends, but the only person I loved with a passion was God. He was the one I felt passionately about, and frankly I thought that the likelihood was that I would never find anyone else about whom I felt that level of passion.

But I was only 20. I thought it would be unsafe and unsatisfactory to go off at that point and become a nun, however much I wanted to. I made a deal with myself. If I had not met anyone else who changed the way I saw things by the time I was 30, I would join a religious order. I was giving myself an opportunity to experience different things. I wanted to understand what I was giving up. I wanted to be tempted, to test my passion for God, because I felt that if I became a nun then I would be Christ's bride and that commitment would be as much for life as any marriage. It would be a once and for all commitment. There would be no going back. I had to know that this was the right thing to do because the consequences if it was not were just too painful and too horrible to contemplate.

So I worked as a barrister and eventually met my husband. We married when I was 29. My life has taken a form that at 20 I never thought it would. I had tried to close doors – 'I'll do anything you say Lord, but ...' – and then He turned things around. I still believe what I am has His fingerprints on it.

There have been moments when my faith has really been tested. These have been when I haven't been able to give things up – like when I thought I couldn't have children. I love children. The work I did at the bar on family law was all about children. I have always had a special affinity with them. I have been surrounded by brothers and sisters and their children all my life. So thinking I couldn't have them after my marriage was the most painful, most soul-destroying thing.

There had been nothing in my life before that I had not been able to pray about. Part of praying, though, is giving it to God. If you give your problem to God, you have to accept His decision. That was why over children I found it so hard. I could pray about not having children, but it was the only time when I couldn't say, for a very long time, 'thy will be done'. If I gave it to Him, I had to accept that His answer to me might be 'no, you can't have any'. I didn't know whether I would be able to accept that.

I was hugging it to myself. I was saying, 'I want what I want and I'm not giving this up because I don't trust You sufficiently'. I was pushed to the edge. I sometimes wonder whether He makes you give up everything, so that the only person left is Him. He scrapes away everything you rely on. And that is the moment when you say, 'Am I a Catholic? Do I have faith? Or do I walk away?' We all hope those moments won't happen in our lives, but there are very few people who don't have them.

It took seven years of praying for me to give it to Him. It was the hardest thing I have ever done. It was the crossroads in my Catholicism. In the end I got to a place where I said 'I've been blessed with a wonderful marriage, a loving family, a good job, children I love in my family. Thy will be done'.

It was like a bereavement – giving up the children I had never had. I went through the trauma and finally I went out and bought myself a two-seater Lotus Elan. I drove it for three months and then started to throw up constantly. I thought I had become averse to the smell of the leather seats. But I was pregnant.

I cannot imagine life without Catholicism. I felt that particularly strongly when my eldest brother died. I adored him. He had been my mentor, someone to whom I felt incredibly close, a soul mate. And then he died at a ridiculously young age, in his 40s. It was like a great big foundation stone in my life had been moved out of the way. It was very painful, not least watching my parents suffer the loss of their son.

His funeral was the first time I had heard the mass in its full beauty. In one way I couldn't bear the words of the liturgy, because each word was like a little drop of blood. I've loved the mass all my life, but on this occasion it was as if I was hearing it – or understanding it – for the first time. There was an extraordinary poignancy that pierced my soul to its core so that at last I understood. The sacrifice and the love. It was all there, and so my pain was immersed in Him until His peace came so softly that it felt like a balm. I remember it as one of the worst and best moments of my life. None of us likes to learn through pain but the truth is we do, and what we learn is the more precious as a result.

I said when I entered the House of Lords that I would never take a government post, but I did. What is central to my Catholic faith is the idea that what God wants for you cannot be taken away from you. You have to accept what He gives. You have to accept that there will be things that may not be what you would have planned. And still you have to walk with Him in faith. I know that whatever I have done as a minister, and will do, it is by the grace of God. I'm not in control of the agenda. My successes are His, but my failures are my own. They come from me.

I realize that putting it in such terms is unusual for a politician, but as a black socialist Catholic in government I am already an oddity anyway. One thing that we grew up with in my family was the knowledge that there was no expectation that we would fit in with anybody. We were accustomed to being the odd ones out.

I refuse to be embarrassed about mentioning my faith in public. I know that some people think 'how quaint, bless her', and that others imagine when I refer to God or prayer that I am speaking colloquially, but they can interpret it anyway they like. I know what I am. You have to be comfortable in your own skin. My faith is what makes my whole life possible. There was one occasion when the House of Lords was being very difficult and so I took my rosary out of my bag and sat on the Front Bench and I prayed. I just thought 'let it go'.

There are, of course, times when I find myself out of sympathy with some of the positions that the Pope or the Catholic Church takes. Maybe it is because I have not taken the obedience part of Catholicism as seriously as I should. Obedience is something I have to learn. I know how little I know, but unquestioning obedience is something I am not good at.

Because there is so much about our faith that is true, and you take it all together, even those bits which are difficult don't make me feel I can renege on the rest of it. If I do, where else is there to go? I don't believe in any of the other constructs.

For me it is about being accepting and working within that Catholic framework, trying to listen to His voice, committing myself to joining in a debate that I might be able to affect, but finally accepting that the only person who can ultimately change it is Him. So I am still a Catholic because, however uncomfortable it may be at times, there is nothing else that makes any sense, nothing else that has any meaning, nothing else that fits together and connects.

More than a Plastic Paddy

Dermot O'Leary, 31, is a television presenter. His parents are Irish but he grew up in Colchester. He started out in local radio and has gone on to present T4, Big Brother, Born to Win, Shattered *and a Saturday morning show on* Radio 2. *He also runs his own TV production company. He has worked with the Catholic development agency, Cafod, and lives in north London.*

I'm like a lot of British Catholics – certainly those of my generation – in that I am constantly questioning my faith, asking why I'm still a Catholic. It tends to come down to a few, very basic questions. Yes, I believe that Jesus died to save our souls. Yes, I go to mass and am a regular communicant. Yes, I pray. Yes, I believe that life is sacred. Yes, I hate abortion and see it for what it is, though I accept that it exists.

Yet, the way I live my life is so far removed from the Church's official position that I sometimes wonder if I can even dare to call myself a Catholic. I use contraception. I'm not married to my girlfriend. I have gay friends. And I don't believe, as the Creed puts it, that there is only one baptism for the forgiveness of sins. Catholicism isn't for me the only true way to heaven.

So I was, for example, very heartened recently when I

read what the Chief Rabbi Jonathan Sacks had written in the first edition of his book *Dignity of Difference*[1] – that there is not Truth, there are truths. That had great resonance for me, even though later he was forced to withdraw the remark.

There are clearly many other ways to reach God, but if I believe there is a God – which I do – then Catholicism is what I've been given to work with. I'm not someone who is going to go shopping around to find a religion that suits my views and lifestyle. I have a healthy distrust of converts to any religion. Invariably they seem to swallow the whole pill and ignore the aftertaste that one gets.

So my own questioning from within Catholicism goes on all the time. Even when I am at mass, there are sometimes sermons when I am so tempted to walk out. Especially when they are all about how evil television is. Or how we should all be going out to evangelize. Yet the frustration has never once reached the point where I would give up my faith.

The toughest battle over the years has been to accept that I have a right to question, that the Church may even be healthier for the questions asked of it by Catholics. There is a whole tradition within Catholicism that says there are rules, it's a club, and if you don't agree with the rules you can use the door. I've slowly come to see, though, that the official Church, the priests and bishops, the infrastructure which can be so conservative and occasionally so scandalous that it drives people away, is not something more important than me.

The Church, I believe, is something we are all part of. Asking us to hand total authority over our lives to the institution has become an unhealthy obedience. Increasingly I have more faith in the idea that I can be guided by my own moral conscience, and through that become a better Catholic. The seeds of that way of thinking came with my upbringing.

Both my parents were born and raised in Ireland. I had that classic plastic Paddy upbringing, back to Wexford in Ireland every summer for six weeks where I'd be bullied in a nice way by my own cousins for being English until anyone else there called me English and then they would stick up for me. We lived in Colchester but I spent every second weekend staying up at my auntie's in Kilburn, the Irish part of London where I live now. There was, and is, a big Irish community there and Catholicism was part and parcel of that. I have often wondered if my Catholicism is more about cultural identity. Am I just hanging on to my cultural heritage? But gradually I have come to realize that there is something more going on.

The way Catholicism was taught at my secondary school was dogmatic, with the result that all my classmates have since left the Church. Although I went through all the same stages as them – catechism classes, first Communion, Confirmation, five years as an altar boy – I now see that what was different was my parents and their attitude to Catholicism. They never made me feel that it was being forced on me. They never once told me to do anything because of my faith. It was never 'get out of bed, we're off to mass'.

They made it a natural thing. And so I quite liked it. I had lots of doubts about the teachings as I grew up, but I was able to separate Church from faith fairly easily. That must have been my parents' influence. They are both self-educated, but well read. They are not liberal with a capital L, but they encouraged me to question. I'd talk things over with my dad more than my mum. And his line was always, 'well you have to make your own mind up about that'. Therefore I never got to the stage of rebelling. If there is a single reason why I'm still Catholic, it's my mum and dad. However, I'm now an adult. So I have choice. God gave me a brain and free will to make decisions. My decision has been to remain Catholic, but not to buy into the whole deal as the Vatican presents it. Like most Catholics in Britain, I'm selective in my following of official doctrine.

What sustains me is the knowledge that beyond the doctrine and the ancient man-made Church laws is something much more important. They simply get in the way of what I believe Catholicism is all about, namely compassion and love. That's the context for my faith. That and the liturgy. The things that keep me Catholic are the importance the Church attaches to forgiveness and its imperative to treat your fellow man as you would want to be treated yourself. It teaches me, at its most basic, to be tolerant, and that when I'm intolerant it is because I'm not the finished article.

Sometimes I come out from mass and for about an hour I'm floating. 'I am a very good person', I tell myself. And then I forget it and find myself being intolerant. Yet, Catholicism does give you something to strive for. You're like a Second World War pilot and they keep raising the number of missions you have to fly before you get to go home. That's what I love about it – the ambition, the idealism, the romanticism. That's what I could never separate myself from.

For me, when you get back to the essentials it is clear. Two thousand years ago a man called Jesus was killed and He was a great man and He did great things. That's where my faith comes from. What He preached I believe. For me, what has come later is the man-made stuff, man's interpretation of those teachings. Too often they have lead to a kind of fundamentalism that still, today, is ruining the bigger picture.

Through my involvement with Cafod, the Catholic overseas development charity, I've been lucky enough to glimpse that bigger picture. I went with them in 2004 to Sierra Leone in West Africa and it had a profound effect on my faith. Back home in Britain, aside from helping people across the road, there's not much you can do in the way of practical Catholicism. There in Sierra Leone I saw this huge level of need and of desperation, and I saw the Catholic faith and the gospel values being put into action every day – the compassion, the loving your neighbour, the love. It was very sustaining.

The way I define my faith is sometimes disparagingly called by others à la carte Catholicism – picking the bits you like from the teaching and ignoring the bits you don't. When I presented a TV programme in 2003 called *Some of My Best Friends Are Catholics*, it was the accusation that the traditionalists I interviewed levelled against me in conversation most often. I wasn't a proper Catholic. There are eternal truths and it is not for us to question them.

I just don't agree. These were people who believed subjectivity is objectivity. The one thing I said back to them was 'yes, I'm being subjective, but we all are'. Whenever you read the Bible, it is always subjective. The Bible can be used to prove anything. So when things are presented by the Church as Bible truth that cannot be contradicted, it is making something objective when it is based on a subjective reading of the text. Now when people tell me I'm not doing what the scriptures say, I have learnt not to get angry but to count to ten and say a pre-emptive Act of Contrition.

I began that programme by being filmed sitting in a confessional and coming out as a Catholic. I've never felt ashamed about talking about my faith, but with some of the statements issued by the Vatican you do occasionally question who in their right mind would own up to being Catholic. In the world of television and radio in which I work, those people who have any sort of religious belief tend to keep quiet. It's not the thing you say. It is surprising, however, just how many Catholics there are in TV. Since that programme was broadcast, I've met plenty of them. They often almost confess their Catholicism to me. I always want to say 'it's not the Reformation any more. You can say whatever you want. It's fine.'

After the programme went out, I got letters that heartened me, especially from young Catholics who said well done for speaking up. There is always another part of me that recoils from such praise because I don't want to be their role model. I'm not setting myself up in any way as a good Catholic. I have, for instance, a terrible relationship with prayer. First I pray when something is going wrong in my life, even though I hate myself for doing it. Then I try to wriggle out by adding at the end 'Lord, I'm not praying to You to make this thing better, but for You to help me with whatever comes along'. I feel like an idiot.

And with my prayers at the end of the day, I start out with the Our Father, Hail Mary, My Little Jesus and a Glory Be, but I keep falling asleep halfway through, so I say an Act of Contrition and start again. And tail off again. I'm like one of those monks in pre-printing press times who were copying out the Bible. They'd make a mistake and have to start all over again.

Invariably those who write to me are quite evangelical in their outlook, and I have no interest either in being a standard bearer in the media for the Catholic faith and all it encompasses. I have never been evangelical. I've never wanted to force my religion on anyone. It's aggressive.

We had a guy on *Big Brother* called Cameron who ended up winning the show. He was a born-again Christian and he had a saying which he used all the time: 'what would Jesus do?' The production team picked up on it and the props girl made wrist bands with 'WWJD' on them. Every time something happened in the house that wasn't particularly Christian, we'd all hold up our wrists and point to the band.

Half the people who wrote in about it knew it was a joke. 'I'm a Catholic and I think it's hilarious.' Others would say 'this is fantastic. It's great to see someone sticking up for the Lord.' And then I got letters from people who thought it was terrible that we mentioned Jesus on television. You can't win.

One of the things about being a questioning Catholic is that I'm always finding myself getting tied up in knots, contradicting myself. So having said that I have no interest in evangelizing others, I simultaneously don't want evangelization to go away. It comes down to me not wanting my Church to be perfect. I'm still Catholic because it isn't perfect. If it was, I'd probably – paradoxical as it sounds – struggle more.

NOTE

1. Jonathan Sacks, *Dignity of Difference: How to Avoid the Clash of Civilizations* (London: Continuum, 2002).

Locked Away Like a Nun

Anne Maguire, 69, was jailed for 14 years in 1975 on charges of running an IRA bomb factory in her north-west London home. Two of her four children were also jailed, along with her husband, brother-in-law and two family friends, collectively known as the Maguire Seven. She served nine years and four months before being released. The convictions were quashed in June 1991, and in February 2005 the Prime Minster, Tony Blair, made a public apology to her and her family. Widowed in 2002, she lives in Maida Vale.

People often say their faith is strong. I used to say it when I was a young mother growing up with my children in London in the sixties and seventies. I didn't know what I was talking about. You can't say your faith is strong until something terrible happens to you and your faith is truly tested. That is when you find yourself confronting the big questions: 'Am I going to turn against God or am I going to keep with God? Am I going to stay Catholic or not?'

My test came when I spent almost nine and a half years in Durham's top-security prison between 1975 and 1984. They put all the worst women prisoners there, and they made sure that I knew I was the worst of the worst. I remember once trying to console another woman inmate when she turned to me and said 'I shouldn't be in here with you because you are the horrible person who bombed all those people'. I can laugh about it now but it hurt at the time.

A lot of things hurt back then. There were headlines in the papers about 'Evil Auntie Annie and her bomb-making factory'. There were neighbours who turned against us once they had seen us on the television news. Looking back I realize they were only human. They listened to what we had been accused of and they thought what a wicked woman to do that, what a terrible mother to involve her children in terrorism.

I kept saying to myself at the time 'if I'm evil, what's good?' I knew in my heart and soul that I couldn't hurt a fly. And I knew that God knew who I was, so He knew that too. In the end that was all that mattered to me.

In Durham I only got out for exercise for an hour a day. For all those long years I didn't see the outside world. I remember thinking most nuns wouldn't have experienced this degree of enclosure. At least they got out and saw people. That's how it felt – that I was a nun locked away, doing a penance. Now we are all sinners. No one can say they're not. So I kept thinking that I must have done something wrong in the past, unbeknownst to me, and that was why I was locked away and was being punished by God. But I couldn't think what it could have been. Everything I came up with seemed so small compared to the punishment.

In the early days in prison, there were times when I couldn't pray. There were times when I didn't want to go to mass. There were times when I even suspected that God had abandoned me. I could have gone either way. In the end, though, it was God who saw me through. That's why I'm still Catholic.

I grew up in Belfast. My father was the one for the

Catholic Church. It wasn't that my mother didn't have time for Church, but her way of looking at Catholicism was that it's a practical thing. If you're a Christian, she believed – and she said Christian, not Catholic – then you help people. Which she did a lot. She never turned anyone away from her door.

The Catholic faith was strong in Belfast. If you have to fight for something, as we did there back then just for the right to be Catholics, then faith tends to get stronger. It was what I was born into. I could never have faith and be anything other than a Catholic, but that doesn't mean I don't respect other people's beliefs.

The way I look at it, you have to be born into the faith – any faith – really to understand it. You grow up with it and it becomes part of you. Nine times out of ten you will continue with it, as I have done. I love my mass. To me, it is like going to see a good film. I just love being there. I feel good in myself afterwards.

I brought my children up in the Catholic faith, but more so, like my own mother, as Christians who knew that they should help people in distress. I look at them now, with their own children and grandchildren. Some of them are still practising Catholics and some are not. If they're not, that doesn't make them bad people. I know that Christianity is still within them.

I got married on a Thursday in September 1957 in Belfast and I sailed for England that night with my husband, Paddy. I was only to come to London for one year to save up enough money to go home and put a deposit down on a house, but I have been here ever since. Paddy had no intention of going back. As my mother said: 'you make your bed and you lie in it'.

I broke my heart because I wanted to go back. I had nobody here living. We were in Maida Vale and I told

Paddy every day that I was going back. Then I had Vincent, my first baby, and I accepted that this was where my husband wanted to stay and bring up his children. We eventually had four – three boys and a girl – and we had a very normal life. Our faith was strong. Paddy was not a religious man but he was a Christian in himself.

There were small things in those years that I didn't agree with about the Catholic Church. I couldn't understand, for example, why you had to fast from midnight the night before if you wanted to go to Holy Communion. If you went to the midday mass on a Sunday, it would be 12 or 13 hours before you'd eat anything. All you could do was have a drink of water. To me that didn't have anything to do with the faith and being a Catholic. If my boys or Ann Marie wanted a slice of toast before they went to mass, I let them. That was different from when I was growing up. So I was glad when that rule was eventually changed.

We were just going about our life when on 3 December 1974 the police knocked on my front door. We were arrested and accused of running the bomb-making factory that provided the bombs for the IRA pub bombings that had recently taken place in Guildford. I found out later that Paddy's nephew, Gerard Conlan, who had stayed with us in the past, had given our names to the police. They believed wrongly that he was one of the bombers and had forced a confession out of him. Gerard's father, Giuseppe, was Paddy's brother-in-law. He was not in good health, but that very day he'd come over from Belfast to see Gerard and was staying with us. He was arrested as well.

We were sent for trial. Paddy and the men were kept in prison while we waited for a court date, but I was bailed along with Patrick, my youngest, and Vince. I tried to live as normal a life as possible, but I kept questioning God. I went to the church most days after leaving Ann Marie at the school. I'd sit and talk and say 'God, why is this happening to me? You know that we haven't done this.' I'd talk to Him the way that you would speak to someone in authority. I always felt as if I got a reply. Each time I'd come away and think it's going to be all right. The truth is going to come out.

So when they announced the guilty verdicts in the courtroom, I just went blank. I didn't want to know anybody – not even God. Everything had been stripped away from me. I wanted to die. I might as well have been dead. They took everything I wanted away from me. My husband and my children were all I lived for. I couldn't understand why God was letting it happen.

Here I was, someone who had never been in trouble before. I didn't know anything about law. And they were saying I was guilty and I was away for 14 years. In my mind I'd never be with Paddy again and I'd never be with my children. They sent my Patrick to prison at 13 and they sent Vince to prison though he was no more than a boy. John and Ann Marie were orphans. That court took my children away from me and gave me them back as adults.

I was ill for the first month or so in Durham and on the hospital wing. I was just out of it. Then two girls, Ann and Eileen Gillespie, both convicted in connection with IRA terrorism, came up to see me and said 'Come on Mother' – that was the start of being called Mother on the wing – 'Come on Mother, you have to make yourself strong.' I said 'who are you? I don't know you.' They told me that they'd got my room downstairs ready, that it was next to theirs and that I must come down.

So they brought me down into the cell. There was a nice spray of flowers on the shelf and a cupboard with things to make tea. That was the start. They were two Christian girls brought up in a good Catholic home in the Catholic faith. They were there for me in my time of need.

It took me a very long time to accept what had happened. I couldn't pray. Even though inside I was praying, I couldn't say the words out loud. I couldn't say 'Hail Mary, full of grace' but inside I could hear myself saying the prayers I had always said. The first Sunday after I came down to the cell, I went with the Gillespies to mass. It was in a room on the wing. No altar, no nothing. I went but I didn't feel anything. I think I was looking for my boys. To me going to mass on a Sunday was having my boys and Ann Marie with me. In prison I was surrounded by strangers. It seemed to be another world. Everything I had done had changed to another way of living.

I carried on going each Sunday but still I was in a daze. A couple of weeks later there was this young priest. In the sermon he said 'there's nobody innocent in prison'. That was the moment I think I woke up from my daze. I remember saying to Ann Gillespie 'did he just say that?' She said 'oh take no notice, Mother' but I couldn't let him go on, so I stood straight up and said 'Excuse me, Father'. He looked surprised and stopped. 'Yes', he said, 'what's your name?' 'I'm Anne Maguire', I replied, and he looked like he'd read about me. 'Yes, that Anne Maguire', I went on, 'the one who has been in the papers as an evil person. You say there's no one in prison innocent. Well I can tell you now, Father, with my hand on my heart before God, that I'm innocent. He knows and I know that I am innocent. And my husband and my children. You have hurt me by saying this.'

'I wasn't speaking directly to you', he said. 'But, Father', I said, 'as a priest you should be careful about what you say because we look on you as our last resort next to God to talk to.' I didn't walk out then. My faith was still there, but I found myself increasingly turning directly to God.

There were things that hurt me about the Church while I

was inside. No one from the parish I had lived in all those years made any effort to contact me. They knew me, but now they didn't want to have anything to do with me. They preferred to believe everything they'd read.

I had no help whatsoever from the Church generally in London, the city where I'd lived for all those years. And the Irish Church didn't hurry to support me. Bishop Edward Daly of Derry came to Durham to visit Ann and Eileen Gillespie but he didn't see me. That hurt, because although I lived in London I was Northern Irish. He must have known I was there. To me that was a bishop from my faith, over from Derry where my ancestors came from, and he didn't want to see me. I think I cried that day. I didn't let anyone see but I was really choked. One or two inmates said to me at the time 'well, if you're a good Catholic, why's he not visiting you?'

Among the prison chaplains, there wasn't much encouragement for my determination to prove I was innocent. Again, here was my Church refusing to help me when I needed it most. There was one chaplain I remember in particular. He was ex-army and I don't think he had much time for the Irish situation. Soon after he arrived we all went to Confession. I went in last and did the usual thing about 'bless me Father for I have sinned', and then I said 'I don't really have anything to confess.' 'That's nonsense,' he said, 'you're in prison.' I thought here we go again and so I said 'yes exactly, Father, I am in prison and I'm totally innocent.'

'No, no, no, let's not go down that road', he replied. 'Well if you don't want to go down that road', I said, 'there's no use in me talking to you.' 'Who do you think you are', he snapped back, 'the Blessed Virgin Mary herself?'

My mother always used to say I was lippy but I couldn't let that go. 'No, Father', I said, 'a virgin I'm not. I've four children, but believe you me I am going through the same suffering Our Lady went through because I'm watching not only my husband but also my children suffering. We've been stripped of everything like Our Lady's son was stripped on the Cross. That broke her heart. And this is breaking mine.'

And out I walked. It was a long time before I went back. I talked to God while I was in prison. My relationship with the Catholic Church was changing.

God was all I had in those years. If I hadn't had my faith, I wouldn't be here today. I wouldn't have come through that horrible time. Faith in Him was His gift to see me through. To come through all that and still love God, and call Him when I need assurance and help, is the most beautiful gift I have been given.

Slowly, prayer came back to me in those early months there. I had a Sacred Heart picture on my wall that one of the girls had given me. I remember lying on the bed in my cell, looking at it. All around it were the photographs of my children whom I hadn't seen for so long. Ann Marie was only allowed to visit me once a year at first. It was the same with the boys, though gradually it got easier. The authorities made me wait for over a year to see Paddy. There were woman on the wing with me who had murdered their husband with the help of their male lovers and they were allowed to see those men more often than I was allowed to see Paddy. Nothing was too bad for us as far as the prison service was concerned.

So I was looking at the Sacred Heart and wondering why all this was happening and why I was apart from my husband and children, and suddenly it was as if Jesus came out of the picture at me and said 'talk to me'. All I remember at the end of it was saying 'right God. It's You and me against the nation. You will give me the strength to come through this – be it one year or ten years.'

Gradually my strength came back to me. I started saying my rosary again. I found the Blessed Virgin Mary a great source of comfort. I still do. I always make sure I have roses to put at the feet of her statue in my local church. I used to say 15 decades of the rosary every day in prison – five in the morning before the cell door was open, five at lunchtime when I had my break and five in the evening when we were locked in. It was something that kept me going. I kept praying that Paddy and the kids would feel the power of the prayer.

And I do believe that prayer is very powerful. I teach that to my grandchildren now. My granddaughter Ellie is five. We pray to the Sacred Heart together. She says 'Secret Heart' instead of Sacred Heart. 'Secret Heart of Jesus, I trust in you.' Trust in God. That's the gift that I'm passing on to my grandchildren.

Prayer kept my mind focused. I did carry on going to mass, of course. At one stage, Myra Hindley came on to the wing. She was younger than me so she didn't tend to spend much time with the three of us who were older prisoners and who would sit talking and knitting. But some of the girls – like Ann and Eileen – said they wouldn't go to mass if Myra Hindley was there too. And Myra was a Catholic. I told them the Devil himself won't keep me out of church.

I'd wait each day for God to answer my prayers, for the wing governor to call me in to her office to say 'there's been a big mistake, you're going home'. It never happened. I started saying to God 'just let someone who is close to You come and do something about this'. First there was Sister Sarah Clark, a wonderful nun who began working for our release. And then Father McKinley and Father Faul from Northern Ireland. Gradually people would start to send me mass cards. I could feel the strength of it building up.

In January 1980 Giuseppe Conlan died and Cardinal

Basil Hume came into the picture. I didn't know him. He'd come as Archbishop of Westminster after we were sent to prison so I'd never seen him. But when he started asking questions about Giuseppe and about our convictions, I don't know what it was. I just felt that this might be the man. I remember looking up at God and asking 'is this the one You've sent?'

God may make you wait. He doesn't just give you things straight away. You may have to wait a long long time like me, but He does answer your prayers in the end. That I firmly believe.

I didn't meet the Cardinal until after my release in 1984. He came to my house. I didn't have two sticks of furniture. Everything we'd ever had had been taken. But I felt it was God Himself who came into my home that day and said 'here I am, you've suffered, you've come through it all, and here I am. I've come now to help you clear your name.' I didn't see Basil Hume so much as sent by the Church, but by God.

With his help we fought to clear our names. That came in 1991, though I had to wait until 2005 for the British Prime Minister to make a public apology to me and my family for what we suffered – and go on suffering.

My parents taught me forgiveness. Never hold anything against anybody, they said. And forgiveness is a central part of Catholicism and therefore of my faith. It is arguably the distinctive Christian virtue.

My mother used to say 'leave those who hurt you to God', and that's what I've done from day one of my release. Even the one who gave our names in the first place. If Gerard turned up on my door, I'd not turn him away if he was in distress. I don't think I'd want to talk to him about the past, but we were all victims no matter who said what.

I didn't struggle with the forgiveness, and I suppose I

should question myself about why I didn't because my children were hurt. I meet people and you can hear the hatred for others in their voices and I think to myself I couldn't be like that. It's a cancer that eats away at them. I couldn't hate everybody who did this to me – the courts and police, even the ones who mocked me when they were interrogating me and told me my daughter was going to be sent to the worst children's home when I was inside. When I think back to them, I still find myself saying 'God forgive them.'

So my faith has emerged strong, my relationship with God stronger. My Catholicism though has changed. I'm still a Catholic and I will always be one, but both the test that I went through and the way the Church reacted in that time have made me see things differently.

I still love the mass, I love a good sermon and I do the flowers in my local church. But with the Catholic Church itself, I tend to do what I feel now, not what the Church tells me to do. I've lived my life, and the way I feel about God belongs to me. I won't be told. That's how I plan to continue. When I listen to the sermon, there are things I don't agree with, teachings I think are wrong, but at the end of the day I just think 'who is going to listen if you say anything?' The people in power in the Church will just go on doing what they're going to do. So I don't bother any more. I sort it out with God in prayer.

Only When I Laugh

Mel Giedroyc, 36, is one half of the comedy duo, Mel and Sue. They have appeared in Light Lunch, Late Lunch *and* The Mel and Sue Thing. *Married with two daughters, she lives in west London and is working on her second novel.*

My early memories of the Catholic Church are vivid and have nothing to do with praying but with laughing. Going to church was a guaranteed source of gags and anecdotes, which to this day are wheeled out if my family is all together for any length of time.

I remember when my two older sisters were put in charge of assembling the Christmas Nativity scene underneath the altar in our local parish church. The afternoon's activities started out as an angelic display of sisterly cooperation, but ended up like something out of the World Wrestling Federation. All you could see were two brown-haired figures tussling and a lot of straw flying in the air. Their theatrical whispering reverberated all the way to the church porch:

> 'I want to do Jesus'
> 'No, I want to do Jesus'
> 'He's mine'

'He's MINE!'
'MINE'

As the papier-mâché Baby Jesu was stretched akimbo, his head was in mortal danger of being torn right off.

My brother used to play the organ a lot and he'd usually draft in one of us sisters to help out. As the youngest, I was in charge of lighter duties like page turning. But my sister, aged 12, was put on the bellows for many months. She used to pump those bellows till she was blue around the gills and in danger of passing out. I can see her now, hunched grimly down near the organ pedals, nowhere near strong enough to provide the wind power needed for Bach's *Toccata*.

My brother was getting heavily into Polish modern jazz at the time and would take great pleasure in suddenly breaking out of the chosen hymn and free-wheeling into a medley of hardcore, incomprehensible riffs which he'd picked up in some late-night Gdansk jazz-hole. When the jazz broke free around the church, Mrs Connolly used to look round from her pew and arch her eyebrows ferociously at him. We'd giggle helplessly when she did, but I mean giggle till we thought we were going to explode, tears coursing down our cheeks. I don't remember ever laughing so much in my life.

Mrs Connolly was one of the pillars of our local church, a leathery woman who had a wide range of flying-suits in her wardrobe and jewellery which was almost equestrian in its size. She would think nothing of wearing a sort of copper halter and pieces of turquoise the size of fairy-cakes strapped to her wrists with leather thongs. She actually looked quite biblical. You could imagine her fending off a shower of rocks hurled by the Philistines.

Her make-up was a thing to behold. Cleopatra springs to mind, as does Dick Emery. Her eye shadow didn't stop at the eyelid; it ascended right up into the brown-pencilled area where her eyebrows once had nestled. If she'd chosen the topaz flying-suit for mass, sure as eggs was eggs, she'd have the coral eye shadow to go with it. It was one of my favourite games on a Sunday, trying to predict which colour she'd be wearing that day.

I suppose my childlike eyes should have been positioned in a slightly more heavenward direction, rather than fixed around me on the motley array of parishioners. To be honest I think I have always seen the church as a performance arena, as much as a place of worship. There are, after all, so many elements of drama to the mass.

Even when I was a little girl, I loved the bits of the mass when I got the chance to go and stand up in front of the crowd. Going to church on a Sunday and to the pantomime at Christmas were the only two opportunities afforded to a seven-year-old in Leatherhead to get up in front of an audience. Mum never believed in ballet lessons or extra-curricular drama groups. She thought them unnecessary and expensive.

It sounds desperately shallow to confess this, but if I had a particular item of clothing that I was really excited about – a pair of stripy pedal pushers for example – what better catwalk to show them off on than the beautiful sweep of carpeted aisle in our local church?

And what is a congregation if not an amazing cast of characters to be observed minutely and then dissected intricately afterwards? One of the reasons I like going to my local Catholic church to this day is that all life is there. Truly it is. The poshies in their twills and tweeds, the parents with so many children that they are blue with fatigue, the giggling kids, the ancient lady in the mantilla, the tinkers, the tramps, the nuns and wannabe-nuns, the terse, the lonely, the thinkers, the stalkers. Sitting at mass in a Catholic church in London is a window on the world, and for anybody interested in character observation, it is heaven. I haven't really experienced the feeling of so many types, classes, mixes of people under one roof whenever I have been present at services in churches of other denominations.

I never went to Catholic secondary school and am convinced that a major reason why I consider myself still to be a practising Catholic is because of this. My brother and elder sister received a very Catholic education but I somehow managed to slip the net. I never ate, drank and slept Catholicism. It was never forced upon me in the way that it can be in Catholic boarding schools.

None of my close friends at school were Catholics. Actually, I have never felt part of a close-knit social circuit of Catholics at any time in my life, either at school or since. Being the only Catholic in my class made me feel rather singled-out, rather special. Of course, we had RE classes, but they were focused on multi-faith teaching, and if anything of a remotely Catholic nature cropped up in a lesson, then all eyes would turn to me, which was a bonus.

I remember the day in 1978 when Karol Wojtyla was elected pope. I felt like a celebrity at school. Having a Polish background and being a Catholic had people rushing up to me at playtime and asking me what I thought of the new pontiff as if I knew him personally. I was half-tempted to sign a few autographs there and then.

When I was 18 I went to live in Rome for nine months. I needed to go somewhere to learn Italian because I'd secured a place at university to study it, and Rome seemed ideal. One of my sisters had tested the waters a few years previously and had given it the big thumbs up. The city made a very intense impression on me right from the start. Even now, when I remember my first days there, I can smell it and feel it as if I were still a teenager again: the crazy posing, honking of scooters, babble of chat, intensity of people's everyday interactions, the warmth of the night air even in February and the bizarrely glamorous and ever-present backdrop of the Catholic Church. It's as seductive and irresistible a place to me now as it was back then.

I became particularly obsessed with the range of shops in the city's back streets which cater to the more earthly needs of priests and nuns. Those tan tights that only nuns wear; you could buy them here by the dozen along with priests' trousers, nuns' nighties, knickers for monks and that particular brand of spongey shoe that I've only ever seen sisters wear: beige or mushroom with an open-toed cross at the front.

Rome's very Catholic environment affected me fundamentally. I found it genuinely amazing to stand on the spot where St Peter had been crucified, to go underground and see with my own eyes where the Christians would have hidden from their persecutors, to walk around the crypt in the Vatican amongst the tombs of the popes. My faith was suddenly put into sharp focus. It felt real for the first time.

My months in Rome were a beguiling combination of earthy and heavenly. I got a job working in a hotel, attached to a seminary and religious house. I was therefore in the rather strange position of working alongside very robust Roman women talking in heavy dialect which took months to decipher (cooks, chamber-maids and so forth), as well as nuns.

The nuns were in charge, they gave the orders and we jumped to attention. The sisters were a combination of Polish, German, Brazilian, Finnish and Portuguese, so the place was a cacophony of miscommunication and disarray. While I was there, a rather overcomplicated telephone system was installed to bring it up to speed with 1980s technology. Bless them, but none of the nuns had a clue how to work this new-fangled, bleeping wonder. There were a lot of eyes upturned and clutching of rosaries, and a lot of flapping wimples whenever its hi-tech buzzing alerted them that a caller was attempting to make contact. It fell to me to work out how to use it and then to operate it single-handedly. It was great for my Italian.

I was bemused and sometimes shocked by the nuns' collective behaviour. I'd never been around women of the cloth together in such tight confines before, and it opened my eyes. They squabbled, gossiped and bitched like a bunch of chorus girls in a West End show. I did my level best to avoid them wherever possible, which wasn't easy in a hotel the size of Fawlty Towers. As I ducked and dived between my various roles of telephone operator, receptionist, waitress and even a stint as a gardener, I thanked my lucky stars that I had never been faced with the dilemma of taking vows. No visitation from the BVM for me in the middle of the night, thank the Lord.

There was a fantastic Lithuanian Monsignor who ran the seminary, whom I sadly encountered not nearly frequently enough. He had a luxurious head of grey hair, Brylcremed to perfection into a towering quiff bigger than Elvis's. His corpulent fingers sported rings to give Mrs Connolly a run for her money. He usually favoured Reactalite sunglasses, indoors and out. I think they eased him into the day when he'd been indulging the night before in his favourite tipple, Bison Grass vodka. In a former life he must have been either a bouncer or nightclub-owner. Yet he was a don of a man, and fantastically combined earthliness with a very obvious and compelling spirituality.

If I ever need to remind myself why I like being a Catholic, I go to Rome. When you're there somehow it seems the natural thing to be. With all its warts, eccentricity and worldliness, Rome is my spiritual home. If I have to die anywhere, it'd be a pleasure to do it in Rome.

Which brings me on to the Thing Which Must Not Be Mentioned. When I was a child I never thought about death except on Good Friday, a day I forever link with having a crashing headache. I found the whole thing so unbearably bleak. Even Mrs Connolly toned down her look, favouring a blue-black flying-suit accessorized with muted pewter bangles. I hated the clackers that sounded instead of the bells, and even though it still afforded me the chance to show off a new pair of shoes or jerkin, I didn't enjoy the terribly self-conscious feeling of having to bend down and kiss the wood of the Cross. It was all so sombre and sad. Why did Good Friday have to come along and spoil my church-going larks?

And why did the congregation get all the rubbish lines in the reading of the Passion? It seemed so unfair. Here I am again, sounding like a disgruntled extra in a film who believes he is destined for much greater things, griping on about his paltry slice of the show-business cake. I so much preferred the Saturday night vigil with all of its pretty candles, and lots of things for the congregation to say and do.

I never used to give death a moment's thought. Death was something that other people did, not me. I, of course, was immortal and was never going to get the grey hairs that my Mum had, or Mrs Connolly hid under her tremendous copper bush. Death happened in films, and yes, I wept many buckets at *The Song of Bernadette*, and as for the film of *Jesus Christ Superstar*, I still start to howl as soon as you see the Jeep cross the desert with the Cross strapped to its roof.

Strangely, the first time I had a whiff of my own mortality was at the birth of my first child. Mixed in with the excitement of this new life force, which had so strangely and violently entered the world, was a feeling that I was on the way out. For real. Not just something that would happen way ahead, some time in the future when Robert Kilroy-Silk is Prime Minister and we've all emigrated to Mars, but actually in the grand scheme of things quite soon. Here was the new generation – this tiny mess of bawling beauty bundled up in my arms. This was the future; I was now part of the past.

This realization occurred two and a half years ago, and I have been to church more times since then than ever before in my adult life. So is it a fear of death that explains why I'm still a Catholic? Yes, partly. I don't want to risk it and do a Lord Marchmain right at the eleventh hour. But it's more than that. It's because now I know that there is so little time left, so little time left to make sense of it all, so little time to say thank you.

I'll admit that my new poncho did get an airing at the early morning Christmas mass, and I still love to watch the characters in the congregation at work, but I now feel compelled to listen a bit more, think and reflect. Life seemed to stretch before me in an endless stream of sun and laughter when I was seven. Now I'm 36 and I still laugh a lot, but it's funny, Good Friday is now one of my favourite days of the liturgical year.

Final Perseverance

IM Birtwistle, 86, is a poet and gallery owner. In the London of the 1940s she achieved great acclaim for her lyric poetry, before moving to Suffolk to raise her three sons. There she started her first fine art gallery, developing a series of young painters into national names. Since 1975 she has run Deepdale Exhibitions on the north Norfolk coast despite, nine years ago, losing her sight.

Catholicism is a great solace at my stage of life, but it doesn't get any more straightforward. As you get older, you reach a point where you realize that if you believe, you must also have doubts. You no longer have black without white. You can't really have belief unless there is, somewhere in the dark regions, an undertow of disbelief and of questioning.

There are days when I never for a moment doubt the existence of Almighty God and Jesus Christ and the validity of the Catholic Church. Whenever the Blessed Sacrament is exposed, for example, I am so aware of the presence of God. It holds you in an atmosphere. You are caught in an element. It is like air you breathe. It's like wind. It's constant. It is just so there. I cannot deny His presence. He's in the host when it is raised on the altar. I know that I am in the presence of something that is way beyond anything this world could produce, an incredible dimension that I cannot necessarily explain, but which I know is the truth.

Part of that truth, if I'm thinking clearly and sincerely, is the Catholic Church, founded by Our Lord, following God's wish. He came to bring to the world Christianity, love and salvation through the death of His Son. And that is what the Catholic Church has always preached. On the way it has inevitably failed and continues to fail miserably, as we all do, but it holds that essential truth. Moreover it stands in direct succession from Saint Peter and can't therefore be anything other than authorized by God. Some of the popes are, I accept, terrifying, terrible men, but whatever the diversions, the main flow represents truth.

I find great comfort in the figure of the first pope, Saint Peter, who was so close to Our Lord, who lived next to Him, worked next to Him, loved Him dearly as a friend, knew Him intimately. Yet it was also Peter who betrayed Him three times as the cock crowed. If he failed, what hope do we have? Yet I find his example consoling. I know we will still be loved at the end of it all even though we make the most horrific mistakes. So we must persevere. My mother's main prayer was always for final perseverance. It used to get on my nerves when I was young as she said it, but now I know exactly what she meant by it.

I struggle more with God than with Jesus Christ. My only way to God is through the Jesuit poet, Gerard Manley Hopkins. He is so profoundly in love with God that it's catching. You can't read anything he's written without being in some way beautifully contaminated by it.

The liturgy of the Catholic Church is remarkable in its understanding of man's deepest psychological needs. Plainchant and all the great wealth of the sung liturgy have fed man's soul down the ages. The late-lamented Latin mass fulfilled a basic need in us for ritual, poetry and

110

theatre, even when we didn't know what theatre and poetry and beauty were. It gave us words and images that nourished a sense of awe, reverence and mystery that told us Jesus was with us, amongst us as we prayed, that we could speak to Him. In this way, the Catholic Church really understood our psychology long before figures like Freud. Other religions have imitated the Catholic liturgy but, for me at least, you cannot make a fulfilling copy out of the original.

Sadly, much has been lost in the new liturgical forms. It was fantastic in the old days. There was a natural rhythm when, for example, you would say three times 'Lord I am not worthy'. In its place today too often we use a kind of media language, something devoid of any spiritual meaning. Because of all these changes, I sometimes feel that I'm still a Catholic in spite of all that has happened in the Church, rather than because of it. I've had to overcome feelings of deep sadness and real distress at seeing the ark that has been given to us for our salvation and our safety pulled apart plank by plank. We seem to have no regard any longer for language, liturgy, beauty and their power to convey metaphysical mystery to anyone with spiritual imagination, to feed that unresolved part of ourselves which no worldly thing can satisfy.

Yet the Catholic Church, for me, continues to represent truth in that it teaches the way to live in a manner that is not always comfortable. It never flinches from it. It doesn't try to dress its message up. So many people today, and so many Churches, try to make palatable a truth that is not palatable by turning it into a non-truth. They don't go along with truth because it doesn't fit. They hedge it with semi-truths.

Of course, I have my bouts of disbelief, usually prompted by terrible tragedies, earthquakes, torture, starvation and the suffering of children around the world. I question why God allows this to happen. The one thing at such times that comforts me enormously is the realization that it isn't God who has allowed it. When the tragedies result from man attacking man, it is man who is responsible. It's our free will. We are not working towards God's will. We are, after all, always praying that God's will be done, which presupposes that it very seldom is.

In these moments of disbelief, I try to remember that we all have a guardian angel. This is another idea that is no longer given any weight in today's Church, but is part of my Catholic upbringing and belief. Our guardian angels are wonderful agents of Our Lord, and are hurt by our failings so often. We make them weep so many times, but they still fight a personal battle with the Devil on our behalf, and at the hour of our death they sweep us up and take us before the throne of God.

My belief, however, does not mean that I follow to the letter everything that the Church teaches. In this regard, I am constantly struck by what an extraordinary thing conscience is. Even in Catholic circles, we rarely talk about conscience any more. I don't know whether it's an emotion, or what you'd call it. For me, conscience is an inner force that is the most dominant part of our lives. We all have this incredible conscience. The child who is not mature still knows the difference between right and wrong. You cannot pretend to your conscience. It is a terrifying voice that is irrepressible. It goes on whether you want to hear it or not.

It has to be an informed conscience. In matters like birth control you can obey an informed conscience. I don't believe, for instance, that women are supposed to produce endless babies. And if they do, and are overworked and swollen with exhaustion, I'd like to see others in their local Catholic community supporting them more. The Catholic Church has got areas that I find unacceptable and unattractive.

I remember as a young woman reading a hardback book called something like *Catholic Doctor*. I nearly gave up my faith on the spot. It was so horrific about women and childbirth – all these ridiculous details about baptizing children before they were even properly born. I couldn't believe that Our Lord meant any of that.

What we have always had to overcome as Catholics are leaders who have become more like bank managers than priests. They have done great damage collectively to the spirit of the Church.

My upbringing was steeped in Catholicism. The Birtwistle family had kept the faith through the Reformation. One Birtwistle was president of Douai in France where they trained Catholic priests in exile. Our house, Huncoat Hall, near Accrington, was said to provide the missing link in a chain of priests' hiding holes running from Stonyhurst across the country. And there was also an Our Lady of Huncoat to whom we prayed as children and still do.

At the time of the Industrial Revolution the Birtwistles lost the faith. It was my mother who brought it back into the family. My father's relatives remained desperately anti-Catholic. There were eight of us children and the rest of the family used to call us 'that papist brood', which in retrospect was the greatest training for us all in ignoring others' jibes about our faith.

We were such Catholic children. Most of our games were played around the Catholic church. In the garden there was an avenue of rhododendrons and we would play catacombs in them. Their great branches made tunnels. So one group of us were catechumens and the other would attack us as heretics. My mother even made my brothers vestments and they used to dress up as priests, hold services in the rhododendrons and give us peppermints in place of Holy Communion.

My father was very honourable about it. He never became a Catholic, but neither did he say anything negative about my mother's Church. He'd take us to mass if she wasn't there. I think he liked the priest more than the local vicar whose living was in his gift.

Usually my mother's absences were because she was having another baby. Each time a baby was born, we'd meet the priest at the door. The eldest boy amongst us would take the bell – which always annoyed we four girls: we only had candles – and ring it gently throughout the journey from the front door to our mother's bed. There we'd kneel down while she received Holy Communion and again ring the bell. And then we'd walk the priest back to the door. This devotion alerted everyone present to the fact that Our Blessed Lord was being taken through the house, so knees were bent in the direction of the bell.

Mass was frequently said in the house. We had many priest friends from Stonyhurst and Ampleforth, including my uncle, Dom Stephen Marwood. He had a profound influence on us all. It was another priest, Dom Bernard McElligott, who persuaded my parents to allow me to go to art school in London in the 1930s.

Growing up with that rich heritage of Catholicism was fantastic. It was the basis of our childhood. My enduring love of the Blessed Sacrament is part of that. We were also brought up on the lives of the saints. It was our bedtime reading and Saint Aloysius was my favourite.

It was also as a girl that I remember feeling the beginning of feminism. My mother was made to walk up the aisle holding the priest's stole to be 'churched' after she had had her babies. I recall sitting there watching with my brothers and sisters and feeling annoyed by it, but not knowing exactly why. Somehow even then I didn't think this idea that women were unclean was quite fair. My mother didn't mind, funnily enough, because it was accepted by her generation.

One of the sad things about the Catholic Church is that it has failed women miserably. It's no good baying on about Our Lady all the time. I have a tremendous devotion to Our Blessed Lady and try to say the rosary every day. I talk to her as one mother to another. I am not a supporter of women priests, but I sometimes feel Our Lady has been used to obscure the fact that the Church has denied women their dignity. Our Lord pointed out a great deal that the Catholic Church has then gone on and ignored. Like Christ's clear teaching 'let he who is without sin, cast the first stone'. Yet in cases of adultery, it is usually the woman who comes off worse. And the Church's treatment of single mothers and illegitimate children has frequently been heartless and without compassion.

To counterbalance such feelings, though, I have been fortunate in my life to come across extraordinary Catholics who have strengthened my faith. Individuals like Frank Sheed, whom I met when I was a student. He was a wonderful Catholic, an Australian theologian, publisher and expounder of the faith. He frequently spoke at Speakers' Corner in Hyde Park from a soapbox. We became great friends. He was a saint – every bone, every beat of his heart was there for Our Lord and the Church. I was privileged to be trained by him, and occasionally would join him at Speakers' Corner on a soapbox.

Today, I would never dare to say that my Catholic faith is strong, because the gift of faith can be removed at any time. You've got to remember it's a gift, and so it can be taken away. That's another reason why I pray for final perseverance.

I visited the Marian shrine at Medjugorge around the time that I lost my sight. Once you've got over the American hysteria there, which is rather off-putting, it is all so moving. While there, I had a strange experience. I was fumbling up a mountainside with my son, Damien, stopping to pray often, when I had this feeling. I suddenly knew for some unknown reason what being dead was like. I'm sure I did. I was transposed into another dimension where I was held, contained, where I felt neither heat nor light nor cold, where I didn't think of anything but the presence of God. I can't explain more than that. I felt that I was totally taken over, absorbed by something that was beyond any kind of reasoning. It was an incredibly happy state, but it was beyond happiness too. It has stayed with me and fortified me ever after.

My Catholic faith is what sustains me. I don't know how people survive without that belief in God, Jesus Christ. I think frequently of the woman who crawled through the crowd just to hold the hem of Christ's garment. If one can achieve that in the end, then one has not lived in vain.

Being blind, you are removed from any kind of life. It's rather like being buried alive if you are an active person. You can never do anything when you want to do it. It happens only when somebody can give you the time to do it for or with you. I'm also removed from the community aspect of Catholic life, although I'm lucky to have local priests who hear my confession and bring me Holy Communion. In this situation, there is something about the Divine Office which gives me a context. I've only come to it recently. I'd been going through what St John of the Cross, one of my favourite people, would call the dark night of the soul. I try to find someone to read the Divine Office to me in the evening, so I go to bed with a clean palate. If you listen to the radio or television your thoughts are certainly not heaven-bound, but the Divine Office is so tranquil, so illuminating and so challenging. It is like going on a pilgrimage, which helps me towards that final perseverance.

This Peculiar Marriage

Charlie Brown, 33, is a journalist and translator. Born in Wolverhampton, he lived in Japan for three years, and is now based in London.

'So, honeymoon over yet?' It is a question that still comes rather frequently my way, usually accompanied by a grin that seems to be longing for confirmation of my regret that I ever became a Catholic. Behind this innocent sounding inquiry seems to be a hope that I'm going to fall to my knees and admit tearfully that it was the worst mistake I ever made. How could I be so foolish to think that I, a practising – if not fully accomplished – gay man, could possibly think that there was a place for me with *them*?

Oh yes, 'them'. Within one small word so much is signified. What an unsightly parade of grisly characters comes marching through the imagination of the normally most rational of people when the subject of Catholicism rears its papist head in the conversation. If only I could have one of those delightfully old-fashioned indulgences every time I am harangued about the Spanish Inquisition, the Borgias and, come to think about it, the granting of indulgences.

Yet none of these dubious moments, or others in the

Church's history, can compete in shock value with a couple of millennia – give or take an admirable exception here and there – of sustained hatred and ruthless persecution of people just like me. So a gay man choosing to become, and then stay, very happily a Catholic really is, as I have been told a few times already, like a Jew joining a neo-Nazi party. Or for that matter, considering the Church's equally shameful record on anti-Semitism, rather like a Jew becoming a Catholic.

It would obviously all be very different if I had been raised in the faith and had had no choice in the matter. I have seen that expression of gentle pity that is given to cradle Catholics at smart social gatherings. It's that look of sympathy which just oozes 'it must have been awful for you'. With a knowing grimace, images are conjured up of terrible childhoods sharing a bed with nine siblings, being beaten – and worse – by drunken priests and mad nuns, guilt, learning interminable catechisms and, for good measure, even more guilt. The assumption is always that all that nonsense is over, a good old lapse has occurred and sanity and health have been restored.

You can imagine then the horror and bafflement when the news is broken that not only am I still very much a Catholic, but that I chose to become one. I can sense the rising disappointment that I cause by coming out of my faith closet and stubbornly declaring that 'yes I am a Catholic, yes I do go to mass regularly and, heaven forbid, yes, I actually enjoy it'. Enjoy being a Catholic? Now that really is kinky. I have often felt like the sort of character you would find in an HE Bateman cartoon – 'The gay man who revealed at an Islington dinner party that he'd become a Catholic.'

So how to answer the inevitable 'what on earth made a gay man like you want to do such a thing?' And the 'and why continue?' My standard reply may sound somewhat trite but I would say that nothing on *earth* made me want to do it. If it had been left to the human institutions of the Church to draw me into its fold, I doubt I'd have come near the whole dysfunctional mess with a liturgical barge pole. Furthermore, if I took seriously some of the hate mail to come out of the Vatican's post box, I would probably be a contender for the record of fastest lapse in history. Rather, in spite of the persistent attempts to deny me and all other gay people a place of authenticity and integrity in God's Church, I have come to realize that those seemingly insurmountable barriers we see before us simply melt away in the presence of Christ.

Through various moments of grace in my life, it is clear that my personal relationship with Him is not dependent on the imprimatur of any priest or theologian, however respected or high up in the hierarchy. And I am sustained in my faith as a Catholic with this realization of the glorious truth that no man – and it is still usually very much a man – is going to come between me and my Lord.

But I'm getting ahead of myself. Perhaps it is best to rewind a little and explain how I got to where I am now. I come from a nominally Christian background, although without any specific denominational ties. Nevertheless, when I was around 14, on the invitation of a neighbour, I started attending the local Methodist church. Strange child that I was, while my peers were behind bike sheds smoking cheap fags and drinking cider, I decided the place to be was down the chapel singing Wesley and listening to thumping sermons.

During these heady spiritual days, confirmation soon followed and it wasn't long before I felt that God was calling me to the ministry. At the age of 17 I first climbed into the pulpit and started preaching on the subject of a world that I had hardly begun to know. I remember though that even then my big theme – if one can have a big theme at 17 – was the enduring love of God, regardless of what we do or who we are.

Even so, it was a time of great struggle with my sexuality and it would be a few more years before I could practise what I preached and accept that love. I came down to London at the start of my twenties and, as the old-time preachers would surely agree, there is no better place to take a boy's mind off all matters spiritual than this city of many diversions. It wouldn't be until I entered my thirties that there would be a drastic shift of my soul's horizon.

It was August Bank Holiday, or to be liturgically exact, the 21st Sunday of Ordinary Time. I found myself, through a succession of events, sitting in a Catholic church in central London waiting for evening mass to begin. I had heard that the priest was famous for his homilies and, even after all these years straying from my Wesleyan roots, there was still enough of a Methodist in me to find this an appealing thought. Besides, I was that weekend at one of the lowest points in my life. I didn't think an hour at church could make it any worse.

Nevertheless I was on guard for anything that might offend those deeply buried Protestant sensibilities. And I thought I found it when we came to the Gospel from St Matthew where Jesus asks the disciples 'who do you say I am?' and St Peter's correct response leads him to the jackpot prize of being the rock upon which the Church is built, and to receiving the keys of the kingdom of heaven. 'Oh here we go', I remember muttering to myself as we sat down awaiting the homily. Cue lots of talk about Peter being the original pope I thought, probably followed by lashings of triumphalism about the One True Church and its fight against apostasy. I braced myself to be condemned as a heretic and then make a swift exit at the end. A lesson from that day: whether it be in a homily, confession or any other dealings with the Church, never make an assumption about what a priest is going to say to you.

I won't repeat everything he said, although I remember his words vividly. Suffice to say there was no rehashing of the glories of Catholic history, no religious hubris and no sense of superiority. There was just a promise that in whatever prison we might find ourselves that evening, Jesus Christ held the key. It is hard to explain but these simple words came crashing into my heart. Suddenly I found that I was in a completely different place from when I first walked in. There were no flashing lights, no choirs of angels, no booming voices, not even, I'm sorry to report, a slight Marian whiff of roses. There was just a knowledge at the very core of my being that my life had changed. I had come back and was now home again.

Slight problem though: this was not by any stretch of the imagination what a Methodist boy – and an out and proud gay one at that – could feasibly call home. I was after all sitting in a Catholic church and a quick look around was enough to remind me that, as Dorothy would perhaps remark to Toto in a similar situation, 'we were not in Kansas anymore'. No, it was quite clear to me that this was merely a means to an end, a divine push in the right direction as it were. It was nothing more than a doorway which would lead, I assumed, inevitably back to my faith roots.

And what could be better for a gay man than the Methodist Church? It has been consistently progressive in its views towards homosexuality and would surely provide me with that community where I could find my home. Yet as the Yiddish proverb goes, 'Man plans and God laughs'. I found a nearby Methodist church and began my re-entry into the Wesleyan world of good preaching, endless hymns and cups of tea.

Yet I didn't quite manage to break the link with the other church. The priest there was after all a very impressive preacher, I reminded myself, and there was no harm in going just for that. I would be Protestant in the morning and a Rome-u-like in the evening. A very – dare I say it – methodical way of balancing a Sunday's spirituality and one which was ultimately unsustainable. It wasn't long before I realized that the Catholic Church was the home for which my soul had been searching.

To put it crudely, it was the mass that dunnit. And it is the mass – along with the witness of the Church in its widest sense – that continues to carry me through those inevitable moments of self-doubt when I look at my Church and ask myself and God what sort of mess I've got myself into. It's why I'm still a Catholic.

It is the centrality of the mass within the worship life of the Church, and its unchanging quality, that is the anchor of my faith, even when I might feel tempted to drift away. Coming originally from a faith tradition where so much depends on the ability of the individual preacher, for example, to make the worship accessible and useful to the congregation, it is strangely refreshing to know that wherever I attend church, it will always be the same mass. Of course, there might be a trendy guitar riff here or incense-spiced Latin there, but leaving these essentially ornamental features aside, in its most basic sense the mass remains unchanged as the *axis mundi* of the Church.

I have tested this theory out in the spirit of classic consumerism with a bit of Catholic shopping around, particularly in the beginning when I feared that it was a priest's good homily or excellent stage directions that was colouring my spiritual judgement. I have church-crawled over London and beyond, attending masses bereft of the warm feeling of community, never mind adequate central heating; I have sat through tedious homilies from the Reader's Digest school of theology, and endured music and singing that would make Charles Wesley turn to drink.

In spite of all this and much more, everything still comes back to the mass and its power to transform even the most meagre and impoverished of worship offerings. Yes, it requires a lot more work sometimes on the part of the faithful in order to approach with reverence a ritual that is not always celebrated with the appropriate mentality. Nevertheless, I find that there is a reflection of our own poverty in the Eucharist which can still be redeemed and be made new. Although I see how over-familiarity with the mass can lead to worship by rote, there is huge comfort for me in what Joyce calls those 'here-we-are-again gaieties'.

There are other sources of comfort that help me to stay the Catholic I am. Just north of Oxford Street there is a famous sculpture by Epstein of the Blessed Virgin Mary and Infant Jesus. It is suspended high up on the wall and Our Lady stands behind Christ with her arms stretched out tenderly (while it has to be said looking rather longingly towards the back entrance of John Lewis). It is a perfect depiction of how the Church is for me when it's at its best – standing back, respecting and encouraging the child's autonomy and freedom to follow the chosen path, however painful that might be to her, but at the same time being there as a constant presence and support whenever needed.

I often stand at the foot of this beautiful statue and give thanks for the blessings that I have received through my Church. It also happens to be halfway between the Methodist and Catholic churches that I first attended and was a sort of station on my literal and faith journey between the two, somewhere I would stop and pray for her intercession that I might be guided as to what I should do. As a Jesuit friend remarked recently: 'you were saying Hail Marys to her statue in public asking whether you should become a Catholic. What bit of the answer weren't you clear on?'

A good point, but one that forgets the main obstacle to my conversion – all the Hail Marys in the world were not going to change what the Church says about me and nor do they completely help in my daily life as a Catholic now. When I first got a copy of that classic bedtime read *The Catechism of the Catholic Church*,[1] rather like a teenager searching out the dirty bits, I went straight to all the juicy talk about disordered sexualities. Ironically, in the edition I have there is a photo of Epstein's sculpture to provide some comfort. Not enough though to block out the knowledge that the high and the good within the Church which I call home see me as nothing more than an aberration of the healthy norms of God's creation.

As I write this, with neat timing I see news of the latest Vatican directive warning the world's diplomats about the grave threat posed by legal recognition of gay relationships. How do I feel when I hear my Church say that? Do I feel like calling the whole thing off and returning to the warm embrace of Methodism? No, not unless the cardinals go there first. Instead, I look at them with all the sincerest love in my heart and say 'we're in this together so you'd better get used to it.'

Fortunately, the catechism and Rome's assorted *bon mots* concerning sexuality are not my only source of spiritual guidance. There are other voices in the Church leading me on through my Catholic journey. Probably one of the most important of these 'kindly lights' is John Henry Newman. It was very early on in my flirtation with Catholicism that the good cardinal entered my life and it was in recognition of his influence on my conversion that I chose John Henry as my confirmation name.

I remember that he first appeared on my spiritual radar with a rather apocryphal sounding anecdote about how his usual drinking toast was 'My conscience first! The Pope second!' Regardless of whether there was any basis for truth in this admirable depiction of moral autonomy, it has become something of a personal motto as a Catholic. Of course, I did come to wonder whether there was such a thing as a theological gaydar when I discovered – to use a certain Anglican archbishop's phrase – what a grey area Newman's own sexuality was. Either that or I'm simply doomed to a life of gay cliché, confirmed when I read his entry in the *Routledge Who's Who's in Gay & Lesbian History* [2] remarking that 'among gay Roman Catholics he is a hero figure'.

It has been this belief in the primacy of conscience and its unparalleled importance within Catholic theology that allows me to reconcile my sexuality with certain teachings of the Church. In times of doubt, when I feel the rage of the Vatican, I am reassured by St Thomas Aquinas' advice that it is better to be true to one's conscience and thus be condemned by the Church than to betray that inner voice in order to toe the dogmatic line. Or I only need to quickly flick the pages of the catechism away from all that talk about sex to find the ringing endorsement that a 'human being must always obey the certain judgement of his conscience. If he were deliberately to act against it, he would condemn himself'. And as Newman stated: 'conscience is nearer to me than any other means of knowledge'. [3]

How could it be anything else? As the guiding force at the very core of my being, it would be impossible for me to ignore it and still strive to be a healthy gay man, never mind a Catholic one. I always knew from the beginning that that inner voice could never be silenced. In the light of that I continue to declare clearly that the Church's position on homosexuality is wrong – just as it was wrong in its dealings with the Jews, women and Galileo. And as with those, I believe that one day it will come to see it is wrong.

Even so, I understand why some accuse me of hypocrisy in being part of a Church whose doctrines I refuse to accept in full. Yet I also know that I will go the grave proud to call it home. Perhaps I am not in an official sense a 'proper Catholic', but then I question whether such a creature exists in the real world. All I can say in my defence is that I fell in love with my Church for all its faults and it's never wise to try to explain fully why we fall in love.

I do know that I would never want to be on the outside moaning about how things could be better. Instead I much prefer working on the inside in my own small way as part of that movement to help the Church become a true and complete manifestation of God's glory on earth.

'You know that if the Church were to admit that it was wrong about gays, it would be theologically disastrous?' one priest asked me after a lengthy discussion. My reply to that remains the same: it was theologically disastrous what the Church did to the Jewish people over the past couple of millennia but it has had to – and still must – face up to the sins committed and make recompense. Theologically disastrous maybe, but for a Church that proclaims the life-giving qualities of the sacrament of reconciliation, it must recognize that there is no shame in admitting mistakes, doing appropriate penance and moving on. There would be no greater witness to the power of the Holy Spirit than for the Church to acknowledge the pain it has caused to some of its most vulnerable children and then transform that weakness into the strength of an all-inclusive community.

Ironically, it is the Catholic faith's ability to look unflinchingly at human weakness without sentimentality or fear which I believe to be one of its treasures. It sees that we are fallen creatures whose poverty – both emotional and spiritual – leads us into all sorts of dark places but it offers a constant invitation back to the table laid by God for us all. For what is the mass but a demonstration of God's power to change that which is broken and human into something perfect and divine?

It is within Catholicism that I have found a space big enough to bring my own weaknesses and failings in the knowledge that even they can be made new. As Julian of Norwich says, 'our wounds become worships'[4] and even those wounds – and I know that to many this is a bizarre if not scandalous thought – those very wounds which are wrongly caused by the Church can themselves by the sacraments offered by that same Church become vehicles of grace.

An important part of my faith is the concept of sacrifice. This is a somewhat unfashionable word in our self-indulgent times but I am particularly drawn to its original meaning of 'making something holy'. Again, it is the transformation of the profane into the sacred – and through God's power using that – which maybe causes us pain to bring us closer to Him. It is also a belief that we can offer up our human relationships in order for them to become incarnations of His love.

This is best manifested in the Church in its widest sense as His body. It is this theology of the Body of Christ expressed in our Eucharistic devotion that leads me to believe that this power can be demonstrated within the relationships in my life, including those of an intimate homosexual nature. It is why I agree totally with the Church's teaching that sex must be 'open to life', but I would suggest that if I and another man come together in intimacy and mutual non-exploitative love, that union *is* open to life. There is nothing more life changing and indeed 'life creating' than the experience of deep unconditional love.

I believe the perfect template for this is the mass. It is a time when a sometimes disordered and unruly group of people with all their hang-ups and brokenness living in their isolated worlds gather together, and through the power of the Holy Spirit and His love become one body which is open to and creates new life. This new life is not only manifested in the changing of bread and wine but also in those present. Likewise, when two men or women meet on that level of love, I see no reason why a whole new blessed creation cannot be born from that experience.

One of the foundations of my faith as a Catholic gay man is the knowledge that at each mass I can witness the power of new life not as some solitary experience but one shared in spiritual intimacy with those around me – even when they are in human terms my enemy. I can be standing next to a rabidly homophobic bigot who may yearn for those simpler days when gay people stayed in the closet – or even better prison cells – where they belonged. Yet with the consecration and the subsequent change that we undergo as the Body of Christ, whether we like it or not the power of that Eucharist overrides all the human barriers and prejudices that we form. This is the miracle of the Church: that we are joined together in intimate spiritual union with those whom even on the best of days we would quite frankly despise.

Each time I attend mass, I am called to 'grow in love with' the Holy Father, the cardinal, all the bishops and the rest of the hierarchy, not to mention the universal Church, which means entering into communion with a sizeable amount of people who are actively doing everything they can to denigrate and destroy my identity as a gay man. Yet what the mass offers in place of that potentially bitter earthly reality is an intimation of the kingdom of heaven where even sworn enemies forget their differences and meet in love. It is the holiness that can spring up out of the most barren and broken of landscapes which is the new song that the psalmist invites us to sing as one.

And it is this entering of communion that I seek in a loving relationship with another man and which will lead to a union that is equally holy and blessed in the eyes of God. We as Christians are a people of an incarnation theology, and none more so than Catholics with our belief in the real presence of Christ. Well, this presence does not just stop at the tabernacle or the altar. Just as His divinity is found in and changes the nature of mere bread and wine, I rejoice that that transforming power can be found in my relationships as much as it is expressed in those of my heterosexual friends. I would even go as far as to say that it is *because* I am Catholic and not in spite of the fact, that my relationships as a gay man have a true potential for wholeness and indeed holiness.

Ultimately though this is not just about the validation and recognition of my relationships. It is at its profoundest level a solid commitment to myself that I belong here in the Church and that there is a place for me as a gay Catholic man. If I just saw the Church in terms of the latest tirade from Rome ranting about me being 'objectively disordered', then I doubt I'd fancy trying to convince the gay men's choir to join me in a rousing rendition of God Bless Our Pope. But as a friend advised, 'remember, the Vatican is just a geographical location. The Church has always been much bigger than the Pope or the Roman curia.' Throughout history we can see how the Holy Spirit has shown admirable stubbornness in His refusal to be put in any neat boxes created by human institutions or authority.

I am reminded of a story told of the great Catholic writer and priest, Henri Nouwen. He was at a dinner when he was confronted by a woman about issues such as the Church's attitude towards women, which she felt might prevent her remaining a Catholic. 'All that is distraction', he replied. 'I don't mean to denigrate or dispute your complaints, but those are beside the point. The only thing that really matters is your relationship with Jesus – I mean a personal relationship with the mystical Jesus.' The woman looked understandably rather stunned and confused by this, so Father Henri continued: 'People complain about the Church, they say the Church isn't interested in their problems. I spoke to a young man with AIDS a few days ago and he told me, "The Church doesn't care about me, where is the Church in my life now when I'm dying of AIDS?" And I said, "Who do you think I am? Who do you think any priest is? I am the Church! And I care about you. That's why I am sitting with you, now."'

There is a community of gay Catholics which meets for worship – some might say rather conveniently – deep in the heart of London's Soho. The mass is celebrated in an Anglican church which is a couple of swings of the thurible away from the gay bars of Old Compton Street. It is a non-Catholic venue due to the usual politics from on high over allowing gay faith to dare speak its name on Church premises.

It is a vibrant community where the Church can be seen in all its beauty, authority and true power. I have taken many straight Catholic friends there and the response has often been similar: 'this is how Church *should* be'. It is a place where there is the brokenness and the deep wounds that many a gay Catholic carries, but there is also the healing and fellowship that springs up wherever the Body of Christ is found. It is through this community that my path became clear and I saw how it could be possible to be a Catholic without betraying either my faith or my sexuality.

And it was with their help that I was introduced to a sympathetic priest – who is now my parish priest – to whom after a lengthy discussion I concluded, 'I feel a huge freedom now'. 'So what do you want to do with that freedom?' was his question. 'I would like to be received into the Holy Catholic Church' was my reply. In one of the happiest moments in my life at the Easter Vigil in 2004, I was finally confirmed as a Catholic. And that sense of freedom has continued to grow and deepen ever since.

So, is the honeymoon over yet? To be honest, I don't think it ever began. I always knew what I was getting myself into with this peculiar marriage and there have been no nasty surprises. Indeed now that I'm a good Catholic boy what else can I promise but 'til death do us part? As a friend said to me once: 'The Church is my mother and she is a whore ... but I love her'. I cannot help but agree. I just hope that she will learn to accept and return the compliment.

NOTES

1. Geoffrey Chapman, *The Catechism of the Holy Church* (London: Continuum, 1994).
2. Routledge *Who's Who in Gay & Lesbian History*.
3. Cardinal Newman. A Letter Addressed to the Duke of Norfolk, 1875.
4. Julian of Norwich, *From Revelations of Divine Love*.

A Work in Progress

Edward Stourton, 48, has presented BBC Radio 4's Today *since 1999 and the religious news programme,* Sunday *since 2001. He has also made both television and radio documentaries on religious subjects, including 1998's* Absolute Truth. *He is currently working on a biography of Pope John Paul II.*

One of the treats of my generally enormously enjoyable job is being paid to travel to places which I would, in the normal course of events, quite happily pay to visit on my own account. Bethlehem in the autumn of 2004 did not quite qualify as a natural tourist destination – the impact of the Palestinian *Intifada* and its associated misery was all too evident in the deserted Manger Square which greeted me on my arrival – but it certainly provided an inspirational starting point for this reflection.

Faith in the Incarnation, the doctrine that God became man in the person of Jesus, has always seemed to me to be a precondition for calling oneself a Christian – although I know that there are clever theologians and bishops who argue differently. What better place to begin answering the really quite difficult question posed by the editor of this book than the town where the Incarnation became a fact of history?

Unfortunately I had brought some seditious literature with me to my hotel bedside in Jerusalem. The case made in Geza Vermes' brilliantly scholarly *Jesus the Jew*,[1] and AN Wilson's biography of Jesus,[2] which is in many ways a companion book to the Vermes work, rather broke the spell. 'The story of the baby being born in a stable in Bethlehem because there is not room for him at the inn is one of the most powerful myths ever given to the human race', writes Wilson. 'A myth, however, is what it is. Even if we insist on taking every word of the Bible as literally true, we shall not be able to find the myth of Jesus being born in a stable. None of the gospels state that he was born in a stable, and nearly all the details of the nativity scenes which have inspired great artists, and delighted generations of Churchgoers on Christmas Eve, stem neither from history nor from scripture, but from folklore. Once we go into the matter, we discover that the real Jesus, the Jesus of history, is extremely unlikely to have been born in Bethlehem. It is much more likely that he was born in Galilee, where he grew up.' Oh dear.

A brief look at your New Testament will demonstrate that AN Wilson is right on the specific point about the stable birth. Does it matter if he is right about the broader point he is making in that passage? It mattered greatly to him, and if I understand his writing correctly his Christian faith has disintegrated as his understanding of biblical scholarship has deepened. But I have not had the same experience. The Incarnation is an absolutely huge fact for anyone who believes it, and the stable story is a remarkably powerful way of expressing the complete inversion of the natural order it implies.

Yet, doubt about the exact location of Christ's birth need not imply scepticism about His existence or His divinity. One of the most attractive qualities of the Christian Churches in general and the Catholic Church in particular is precisely the way they use stories like the Nativity to illuminate the truths which lie at the heart of their teaching.

Catholics have more of these stories than most. Some of them – particularly those about the saints – are of the Harry Potter variety. As a teenager I remember being greatly taken by Vita Sackville-West's life of St Teresa of Avila, a fastidious and flirtatious sixteenth-century Spanish aristocrat who seems to have resented her call to holiness and suffered dreadfully from involuntary levitation; she sometimes had to hold onto the altar-rail at mass to stop herself taking off. A huge crowd gathered for her funeral, and she is said to have been so distressed by the smelliness of the populace that she fluttered out of her coffin into the cathedral rafters, refusing to come down until they had dispersed.

At Ampleforth, the Benedictine monastery where I was educated during those formative teenage years, there was a curtained niche to the right of the high altar in the Abbey church which was said to contain a charred bit of St Lawrence. St Lawrence was barbecued on a gridiron during the Valerian persecution of 285, and he is reported to have uttered last words of impossibly heroic irony; '*Assum est, versa et manduca*' – 'I am done on that side – turn me over and then you can eat me'.

Stories like these give Catholics a sense of living in a world into which God pokes His nose on a regular and often eccentric basis, and they provide a purchase for us to grapple with our sense of the numinous in what we see around us. There are other more profound stories – like the Nativity – which seem to speak to archetypes lying deep within the human soul – or psyche, if you are disposed to give it a more neutral designation. And the way they have been developed and embellished by art over the centuries has given many aspects of Catholic culture a universal appeal.

On some of my visits to St Peter's in Rome, I have felt exhausted by the triumphalist papist grandeur of the place, but if you retreat to the back of the basilica and watch people looking at Michelangelo's *Pietà* you can refresh yourself with a simpler and purer experience; the statue is much more than a pious retelling of Mary's moment at the foot of the Cross, it is an image of mourning motherhood that every human being can understand.

To many Catholics, monuments like the *Pietà* demonstrate that all human life can be explained by being viewed through a Catholic lens. But Catholicism at its best and most cheerful accepts a humbler role; you can renounce the Church's doctrines and still use the art they have inspired to help make sense of the human condition. That is why, despite all that guilt and penance, and the disciplines that demand denial, Catholicism is a life-enhancing religion in a way some of the greyer and more puritanical forms of Protestantism can never be. Catholic culture is woven out of the things that make this life worth living – visual beauty, inspiring music, wine and well-chosen words prominent among them.

From my own experience I know a little about how tough Church discipline can be. I am divorced and re-married, and have therefore excluded myself from the sacraments. Some of those who read this may feel that I should not be writing it at all, because I am not, strictly-speaking, in communion with the Catholic Church; I can only apologise if they are offended, and would simply say that my fundamental Catholic beliefs remain as they always were.

My position makes it quite impossible for me to contribute to the debate on whether Catholic teaching on marriage and divorce should change. By the same principle that meant Richard Nixon had to open up American relations with China and that only a Conservative leader like Margaret Thatcher could compromise over white rule in Rhodesia, any change in that area will have to be championed by the crustiest celibates. But losing my right to take a full part in the Church's life has given me a new understanding of that Catholic 'clubbiness' which sometimes repels outsiders.

I was born into the clubbiest bit of the club. My family were 'recusants', which meant they refused to abandon their Catholic faith despite the persecutions Catholics suffered under the Tudors and Stuarts. Formal penalties against Catholics continued until the Catholic Emancipation Act of 1829 – and anti-Catholic prejudice, of course, persisted long after that. So for several centuries the recusant families huddled together, endlessly intermarrying to create one huge 'cousinhood', their sense of their Catholic identity steadily sharpened by the shared experience of persecution. Since the families tended to be rather grand, most of this huddling took place in large country houses, and there were definitely social as well as religious requirements for club membership.

This curious cultural cocktail was further complicated by a strong cult of martyrdom. The English Martyrs who died for the old faith include 42 full saints, 221 blesseds and 30 venerables; many were priests who trained in the beautiful English College just off the Piazza Farnese in Rome, returning to serve the faithful from the secrecy of priest holes before being caught and executed.

Of course, they had their Anglican counterparts – those who died at the stake under Bloody Mary – but somehow being martyred for the winning side does not quite cut the mustard in the same way. The memory of the Catholic English Martyrs is kept vividly alive in English Catholic schools and churches. Palestinians in the West Bank and Gaza have a practice of sticking up posters of suicide bombers and people who have been killed in Israeli attacks to sustain the cult of martyrdom which has become such a significant factor in their conflict. I suspect I am alone among my journalist colleagues in finding myself reminded of my prep school by this habit; most of our dormitories were named after people who died in the most disgusting ways several centuries ago – being hung, drawn and quartered was an exceptionally horrible death – and the propaganda purpose was precisely the same.

I have a book called *Blood of the Martyrs*, which somehow symbolizes the determination to preserve recusancy as a living tradition. It traces the blood lines of some of the most prominent English Martyrs and informs me, at the bottom of a long family-tree much adorned with heraldic devices, that I am descended from St Philip Howard, an Earl of Arundel who was condemned to death in 1589 for having mass said in his cell in the Tower of London.

With such impeccable membership qualifications it came as a shock to have my club card withdrawn when I became a re-married divorcee, but it was also rather salutary, and caused me to reflect on the tension in Catholicism between its exclusivity and its aspiration to be a universal, truly catholic Church. The tension is there from the Church's earliest days. St Paul sometimes reveals himself to be the most vengeful club secretary, determined to expel anyone who has infringed against the by-laws. He tells the Corinthians that they should not 'associate with anyone who bears the name of brother or sister who is sexually immoral or greedy, or is an idolater, reviler, drunkard or robber. Do not even eat with such a one ... Drive out the wicked person from among you.'

Yet his letters are full of tenderness and affection for those within his new churches, and they convey a sense of real excitement about discovering a new network of associations which stretched right across the Roman Empire, linking people not by the old ties of race and tribe but by a new tie of shared faith. I have felt proudest about my Catholic badge when I have seen how effectively the Church's beliefs and rituals can transcend race and culture; when I have found myself just as much at home at mass in India or Africa, for example, as I would be at a service in Westminster Cathedral. But of course that very sense of 'belonging' is itself exclusive.

Much of the Church's history is the story of a continuing debate about precisely that kind of dilemma, and despite its reputation for bone-headed obscurantism when confronted with the need to change, Catholicism does in fact have a dynamic quality. It would be rude of me to question the title which the editor of this book has chosen, but I detect a whiff of prejudicing the argument in the use of the word 'still'; it suggests a 'despite' in the sub-text, a conviction that we apologists must make our case in the face of overwhelming evidence of the general ghastliness of the Church under the long reign of John Paul II.

I have chosen not to address the difficult subjects for the Church's champions for the simple reason that I think the Vatican's position on some issues – contraception in the battle against AIDS being the obvious example – is indefensible. But it is worth saying something about the institution of the papacy, because it need not always be the conservative force it has been of late. Unlike some forms of Islam and evangelical Christianity, Catholicism does not make a fetish of its texts; it holds that scripture is necessary for an understanding of the truth, but not sufficient; the Church exists to help us interpret the will of God.

I would take that a stage further and argue that religion is always a work in progress, and that it is our constant duty to use our God-given talents to discern His will and meaning. The papacy is essential to that process, because it can provide the leadership necessary when the Church develops its thinking or – whisper this, but it does happen – changes its mind. The Second Vatican Council in the 1960s provides the obvious example of a revolution led from the top. This is, I know, a very Whiggish view of Church history – and one which would certainly not find favour in today's Vatican.

Much of the argument I have made here could probably be advanced by someone calling themselves a 'cultural Catholic', an increasingly common expression for a person who feels soaked in the Catholic ethos but does not actually believe in God. An agnostic or atheist can appreciate the power of Catholic art and myth making, admire the universality of Church's sense of mission, and perhaps even give some credit to the Vatican as a source of moral leadership. Catholicism is such a fascinating and important part of our history that it is perfectly possible to write about it at great length without mentioning God at all, and there have been plenty of people who have risen to the top of the institution without spending very much time thinking about Him.

However, I have found that God has come to occupy a surprising amount of my energy in my professional life as a broadcaster. That is partly because religion has a more and more significant place in the news agenda – something I suspect very few people in this country's highly secular elite would have predicted a few years ago – but also because He continues to preoccupy many of my colleagues in their private thoughts. My fellow Radio 4 presenter John Humphrys, an atheist, frequently takes me to task over the eternally compelling question of His existence, usually while the *Today* programme is on the air.

John's argument – eloquently developed but occasionally

interrupted by the necessity of interviewing a cabinet minister or introducing *Thought for the Day* – is a familiar one among journalists; most of us have seen rather more than our fair share of human misery in the course of our working lives, and if you spend enough time contemplating the caravan of human suffering that rolls before our eyes you cannot avoid asking why an all merciful God does not shout 'Stop!' from time to time.

On a memorable occasion John was able to put that question to someone much better qualified to answer it than I could ever be. He persuaded the Archbishop of Canterbury, Rowan Williams, to be interviewed after the end of the school siege at Beslan in southern Russia, a massacre of the innocents if ever there was one. 'Where', John asked the archbishop, 'was God yesterday morning?'

Dr Williams was appealingly modest in the theological ambition of his answer; he asked us to imagine an older child putting his arms around a younger one amid the maelstrom of bullets that erupted within the school gym and suggested 'you might find God there'. That sort of God is very different from the often avenging and sometimes cruel figure of the Old Testament, but I find Him convincing, and perfectly compatible with the teachings of the Catholic Church. John was worried afterwards that the interview had failed because it was so personal, but it had of course succeeded triumphantly precisely because he was asking the questions for himself.

If you believe that real religion is a process rather than a condition, as I do, it can become exhausting; it means nurturing doubt and questioning anything that looks remotely like an easy answer. But as my middle age marches on I have found myself becoming less and less energetic about challenging the habit of mind that faith has become. Perhaps it is just the advancing years, or perhaps this intellectual sloth is a kind of grace, something I should accept as a gift from God. With a bit of luck it will not at any point involve involuntary levitation or making witty remarks while being cooked like a fast food.

NOTES

1. Geza Vermes, *Jesus the Jew: A Historian's reading of the Gospels* (London: Collins, 1973).
2. AN Wilson, *Jesus: A Life* (New York: Ballantine Books, 1993).